MW01601317

North Korea's Nuclear Gambit

Understanding Pyongyang's Survival Strategy

STRATFOR
GLOBAL INTELLIGENCE

STRATFOR
221 W. 6th Street, Suite 400
Austin, TX 78701

Copyright © 2011 by STRATFOR
All rights reserved, including the right of reproduction
in whole or in part

Printed in the United States of America

The contents of this book originally appeared as analyses
on STRATFOR's subscription Web site.

ISBN: 1461068681
EAN-13: 9781461068686

Publisher: Grant Perry
Editor: Michael McCullar
Project Coordinator: Robert Inks
Designer: TJ Lensing

CONTENTS

CONTENTS

ILLUSTRATIONS

INTRODUCTION

The Hermit Kingdom, a charter member of the Axis of Evil, a black box, a rogue regime. North Korea remains one of those places everyone knows about and no one knows about. It is seen interchangeably (and sometimes simultaneously) as an unpredictable and dangerous nation with stockpiles of chemical and biological weapons, nuclear weapons and long-range ballistic missiles under development, an expired regime, a hollow economy and a starving population. It is, in short, a place seen as dangerous and weak, an enigma of a country on the verge of collapse. And this may be exactly the image North Korea intends to portray.

Squeezed between China, Russia, Japan and South Korea — and U.S. military forces in the latter two countries — North Korea sits in an uncomfortable geographic position. Following the Korean War, North Korea survived on handouts from the Soviet Union and People's Republic of China and learned rather quickly to play the differences between these two ostensible bloc allies to Pyongyang's advantage. As the end of the Cold War neared, North Korea was highly attuned to the changing winds. China was looking to South Korea, Japan and even the United States as partners in its accelerating economic reform and opening up. Russia was trying out perestroika and glasnost in its own attempt to forestall economic catastrophe. And in the midst of all this, North Korea was being left behind, seen as more of a liability than a benefit for these two regional powers.

Pyongyang did not, however, move into this new world unprepared. In the 1980s, then-leader Kim Il Sung laid the groundwork for a new survival strategy, one that used a global fear of nuclear proliferation, particularly from the United States, to strengthen Pyongyang's position. When the first nuclear crisis emerged in 1993, it was not about North Korea being caught at something secret and chastised by the international community; it was the first in a series of choreographed moves by Pyongyang to reshape the box it was in. By 1994, Pyongyang had moved from a position of weakness as a remnant of the Cold War to a position from which it could actually influence U.S. behavior. North Korea had become the center of attention.

The plan at the time was to use the fear of a potentially nuclear North Korea to press the United States and other countries into giving concessions, aid and assistance to North Korea. It was about survival, replacing the Chinese and Soviets with the United States, Japan and South Korea as the suppliers and, in effect, guarantors of North Korean survival. It was an interesting twist, one that seemed anathema to the western perceptions of North Korean ideology but fit rather nicely with the longer-term view of Korean history and its constant struggle to balance between the larger powers all around. 1994 was supposed to be the year of the first inter-Korean summit, and it is interesting to speculate what may have happened if Kim Il Sung hadn't died suddenly while preparing for South Korean President Kim Young Sam's visit.

It took Kim Jong Il more than three years to solidify his rule, even after years of it being clear he was the chosen successor. In August 1998, the younger Kim added a new twist to the still-simmering nuclear crisis, with North Korea's first long-range missile test. Within two years, then South Korean President Kim Dae Jung was in Pyongyang to meet with Kim Jong Il, North Korea had expanded its diplomatic relations through Europe and Asia, and North Korea was again reaping the benefits of its survival strategy. The apparent feelings of camaraderie lasted a little while, and then Pyongyang fell back onto the global blacklist, only to build up to the next cycle of crisis and compensation.

Over and over again, North Korea has employed the same basic strategy:

- Take steps that are seen as threatening by the United States, North Korea's neighbors, and the international community.

- Appear rather unstable and unpredictable internally — be sure that it appears you may be just crazy enough to use these weapons if you are pushed.

- Let the world know how close to collapse you are, due to food shortages, economic mismanagements and a failing infrastructure.

The elite in North Korea do not have any interest in giving up or fundamentally altering their power structure. True economic and political reform is just not an option — they have seen the result of such moves in the Soviet satellite states and in the Soviet Union itself. The country also truly wants to avoid another war. The Korean War was devastating to North Korea, and any future war will result ultimately in North Korea losing. Pyongyang projects an image of fearsomeness to pre-empt any real thoughts of a military solution to the North Korean problem — the cost to South Korea alone would be devastating, and the longer the range of North Korean missiles, the more Japan, China or even potentially the United States would need to worry about the final salvos of a state with its back to the wall. Pyongyang has learned that it is better to be feared than completely ignored.

The final stage is to allow the impression of both domestic weakness and unpredictability of the elite. In short, North Korea appears a nation on the verge of internal collapse, starving citizens fleeing across the border, malnutrition rampant. But this weakness doesn't mean regime collapse; rather, the impression Pyongyang gives is that the regime would become less predictable the worse things got at home. In other words, it is in the interest of the international community to bail out North Korea, to prevent the collapse, because what comes next could well be worse than what is now.

This book traces several steps in Pyongyang's careful manipulation of its image, and its ability for the most part to play a fairly strong hand despite weak cards. The strategy has served North Korea for more than a decade and a half, but the problem is that the longer they play this game, the less responsive the world is. The threshold of action Pyongyang must take to instigate a sense of imminent crisis, and thus force the hand of the other players, is getting higher and higher. No longer is it sufficient to test a rocket, or allow a satellite to image a new North Korean nuclear facility. Even testing a nuclear device seems too small to stir a sense of imminent doom. If the sinking of the ChonAn and the shelling of Yeonpyeong Island doesn't force an immediate response, just how far will North Korea have to go?

Rodger Baker, VP, Strategic Intelligence
STRATFOR
Austin, Texas
April 4, 2011

A NOTE ON CONTENT

STRATFOR presents the following articles as they originally appeared on our subscription Web site, www.STRATFOR.com. These pieces represent some of our best analyses on North Korea's survival strategy since 1999, presented in the order in which they were published. Since most of the articles were written as individual analyses, there may be overlap from piece to piece, and some of the information may seem dated. Naturally, many of the observations herein are linked to a specific time or event that may be years removed from Pyongyang's situation today. However, STRATFOR believes bringing these pieces together provides valuable insight and perspective on a significant country.

NORTH KOREA

RUSSIA

CHINA

NORTH KOREA

East Sea/Sea of Japan

West Korea Bay

Pyongyang

SOUTH KOREA

Seoul

0 mi   50   100
0 km

Copyright STRATFOR 2011   www.STRATFOR.com

North Korea and the End of the Post-Cold War World
March 22, 1999

Last week, the United States and North Korea announced a breakthrough agreement permitting the United States access to North Korean nuclear reactors. The agreement appeared to signal a significant improvement in atmospherics in the region. Japan and South Korea, however, made it clear that they were not yet prepared to allow the atmosphere to improve. At a summit in Tokyo on Saturday, Japanese and South Korean leaders indicated that the level of distrust between them and Pyongyang was still extremely high. South Korean President Kim Dae-Jung told a news conference in Seoul that "We must tell the North that it would be the North which would suffer massive damage if it launched [a] provocation."

More important than atmospherics, Kim told reporters that he and Japanese Prime Minister Keizo Obuchi had agreed that Tokyo and Seoul should join with Washington to create a tripartite agreement on responses to any use of weapons of mass destruction (WMD) by North Korea. Obuchi softened Kim's statements somewhat by emphasizing that he endorsed Kim's "Sunshine Policy," which sought to shift North Korean behavior through a process of engagement, particularly focusing on bilateral economic arrangements, designed to make peaceful cooperation more attractive than isolation or war. At the same time, while taking a mildly different tone, Obuchi made it clear that he is prepared to join in a trilateral military alliance.

In an interesting related development, Japan's Asahi Shimbun reported that the United States would conduct evacuation drills in

South Korea next week. A key problem facing the United States in Korea is the evacuation of tens of thousands of non-essential or non-military personnel in the event of war. Asahi has reported that a small-scale exercise testing the ability of the United States to rapidly evacuate these personnel in time of war will be tested. This report immediately triggered a North Korean warning that the United States was bringing the peninsula closer to war.

These odd crosscurrents are precisely what North Korea is hoping to generate. As we have stated before, we see North Korea as pursuing a consistent, rational foreign and defense policy ever since 1991. The collapse of the Soviet Union and the shift of China toward integration in the Western economic system left Pyongyang completely isolated in 1991. There was a general expectation that the North Korean regime could not survive and serious contingency planning was undertaken in South Korea and elsewhere to determine courses of action in the event of a North Korean collapse. North Korea was fully aware of this planning, fully aware of its isolation, and fully aware of its vulnerability. It designed a policy to avoid what appeared to be an inevitable fate.

This policy consisted of two parts. First, North Korea did everything possible to make it appear that it was economically in dire straits and therefore on the verge of internal collapse. North Korea took real problems in food supplies and food shortages and made them appear to be outright famine. There was method in their madness. By convincing South Korea and the United States that economic collapse was imminent, the North Koreans dissuaded both from taking direct steps to worsen the situation in the North. By painting the situation in the North as desperate, they convinced South Korea and the United States that no further tightening of the noose was needed. Thus, instead of seeing the economic noose tightened at a time when neither Russia nor China would raise a finger to come to its aid, North Korea convinced everyone that with collapse so close, further action was superfluous.

North Korea went one step further. When South Korea and the United States began to think through the consequences of a complete economic and political collapse in North Korea, they realized that a rapid, unexpected collapse would pose greater problems than might be imagined. Who, for example, would be responsible for North Korea's debts on the international markets? Who would be responsible for preventing starvation and disease? The North Koreans created an atmosphere in Seoul and Washington in which it was assumed that Pyongyang's collapse was inevitable and in which contingency planners found that delaying North Korea's collapse until a more opportune time, or at least until more comprehensive plans were in place, would not be a bad idea. Seoul and Washington, thinking about a sudden and uncontrolled collapse, actually started to pursue policies designed to cushion the landing. This was perfect from Pyongyang's approach, buying time and more than a few resources.

If Pyongyang's first strategy was to convince everyone that pressure was not needed to cause North Korea to collapse, thereby buying North Korea desperately needed breathing room, then the second stage of the policy was to convince the world that North Korea retained the military capability to cause frightful problems if it were pressed too hard. This policy consisted of two discrete stages. In the first stage, running the first half of the 1991-1999 period, the emphasis was on North Korea's conventional threat to the South. North Korea staged constant military exercises along the DMZ, many frightfully realistic. It carried out extensive special operations and generally maintained a level of military tension short of seriously threatening war but never leaving anyone in peace.

The second part of the strategy was to seriously pursue weapons of mass destruction. The goal was the same as with conventional warfare: to create a general sense of insecurity without triggering a response. Two valuable results flowed from this policy. First, fears arose in the region, and even in the United States, about North Korea's ability to unleash weapons of mass destruction. The goal was not necessarily to build these weapons (although that was desirable) but to create a general uncertainty as to whether these weapons had been built. That uncertainty would limit outside efforts to destabilize the regime and deter military operations. A second outcome was that it compelled

South Korea, the United States and even Japan to try to find "carrots" with which to dissuade North Korea from developing and using those weapons.

In other words, if North Korea might have weapons of mass destruction, then using sticks on North Korea was extremely dangerous. This meant that only incentives could be used, which was precisely what North Korea wanted in the first place. The incentives helped stabilize North Korea's economy. In effect, the two strategies flowed together. In schematic form, here is what happened:

- North Korea finds itself isolated and vulnerable.
- North Korea convinces the world that it is on the verge of collapse.
- North Korea is believed and steps are taken to cushion the fall.
- North Korea convinces the world that being on the brink of collapse and in the grip of an irrational ruling class willing to do anything to survive means that any action by outsiders designed to hasten that decline could lead to dangerous and irrational behavior on North Korea's part.
- North Korea convinces the world that it may have weapons of mass destruction capable of destroying Seoul, Tokyo and, who knows, Los Angeles.
- North Korea bluffs adversaries into providing more resources.

As a result, rather than isolating and strangling the North Korean regime, South Korea, Japan and the United States become obsessed with dissuading the North Korean regime from using its weapons of mass destruction. Since the North Koreans are irrational and desperate, nothing must be done to frighten them into action. The regime's survival must not be an issue. The only threats made against North Korea are directed against its weapons of mass destruction. Sunshine Policies are pursued to stabilize the North Korean government and convince them that cooperation is more profitable than conflict. The three significant powers, the United States, Japan and South Korea, confine their threats to the use of WMD, while indicating that they are open to economic relations.

The winner is North Korea, game, set and match.

The only thing that North Korea wanted to do was to survive until the international climate shifted. Extensive Russian and North Korean talks were held last week. China and the United States are rapidly moving toward hostility. Suddenly, North Korea may not remain isolated. Certainly, no one is planning any longer on a sudden collapse in Pyongyang. Summit meetings are held to meet the North Korean threat and to continue the policy of constructive engagement. So long as the issue on the table is whether North Korea will or won't attack, North Korea has won, because the issue on the table is not whether North Korea will survive.

North Korea is a perfectly rational state that has no intention of using its weapons of mass destruction, assuming it has them. It wanted to persuade the world that it was, sequentially, weak, crazy and deadly. It has done that. Now, as the world shifts from the post-Cold War world to the post-post Cold War world, the real issue on the North Korean agenda is developing good relations with Russia and China. Let South Korea, Japan and the United States obsess over North Korean weaponry. The real issue for North Korea is mutual defense agreements with Moscow and Beijing. North Korea liked the Cold War. Seoul, Tokyo and Washington are obsessing over the last era's issues. They are missing the emerging issue.

The Return of the 'Crazy Fearsome Cripple'
Dec. 23, 2002

North Korea has begun removing International Atomic Energy Agency (IAEA) seals and cameras from its nuclear facilities prior to restarting its frozen nuclear program. Pyongyang began removing the seals after it accused the IAEA of ignoring an earlier request to do so itself. The action has triggered alarm in the region and in the United States, where officials suggested North Korea could produce an additional half-dozen nuclear bombs in a matter of months.

Pyongyang's removal of the seals is just one more step in a series of provocative statements and acts involving North Korea's nuclear and missile programs. The North Korean government has spent years preparing for a confrontation with the United States in 2003 — hoping to pressure Washington into a new round of negotiations. Washington's current preoccupation with terrorism and Iraq would seem only to benefit North Korea's strategic calculus.

But Pyongyang's carefully planned "shotgun wedding" approach to dealing with the United States is predicated on more than just a desire for talks. The regime's primary concern is survival, and Pyongyang feels increasingly abandoned by former allies and supporters China and Russia. And, as it did in the early 1990s — when Moscow and Beijing offered diplomatic recognition to Seoul — Pyongyang feels compelled to act swiftly.

Over the past few months, North Korea has stepped up its diplomatic engagement with Japan and South Korea while simultaneously dropping hints that it is fed up with the United States and the lack of progress in talks with the Bush administration. North Korea has, in the following order, threatened to restart its plutonium-based nuclear program, hinted that it has a new uranium-based nuclear program, announced the re-launch of its nuclear program, called on the IAEA to remove seals and cameras in its nuclear facilities and, now, begun to remove those seals itself.

Pyongyang also has suggested that it might restart its missile program. The government then told Japan it would extend its moratorium on testing long-range missiles, only to again defend its right to possess and test long-range missiles. The moves on both the nuclear and missile programs are part of a combined strategy to present a potentially dangerous image of a nuclear-armed North Korea capable of delivering warheads to the continental United States. This, Pyongyang posits, will convince Washington that it has no choice but to sign a non-aggression treaty with North Korea, or even move toward formal peace negotiations and diplomatic relations.

Pyongyang chose 2003 for a confrontation with the United States for several reasons. The first is symbolic: The year marks the 50th anniversary of the signing of the armistice that ended the Korean War. Second, it was to be the completion date for the internationally funded light-water nuclear reactors that the United States and others promised to build in return for Pyongyang ending its nuclear program in 1994. Third, 2003 marks the end of Pyongyang's self-imposed moratorium on testing long-range missiles. Finally, a new president will take the reins in South Korea early next year.

The attention that Washington currently is focusing on the war against terrorism and on Iraq only adds to North Korea's interest in pressing its case as 2002 winds down: Pyongyang considers the U.S. government unwilling and unable to allow another international security crisis to erupt at this time.

Yet far from acceding to Pyongyang's demands, Washington continues to both ignore and isolate North Korea. While a more permanent peace accord with Washington would be a major political — and potentially economic — coup for North Korea, Pyongyang's primary concern is the survival and perpetuation of the regime. And it is a sense of isolation that has pushed North Korea along its current provocative path.

Over the past year or so, China and Russia have distanced themselves from Pyongyang and focused on other pressing issues, ranging from internal political transitions to ties with the United States and Europe. North Korea has remained a side issue for both nations — and Beijing in particular has grown weary of North Korea's failure to consult it before making economic and political decisions that impact China.

And when North Korea feels isolated — even by its so-called allies — it shifts to a strategy that STRATFOR has dubbed the "Crazy Fearsome Cripple Gambit." In essence, it is a three-pronged strategy designed to gain time for the regime and to create rifts in the

7

trilateral coordination among Seoul, Tokyo and Washington, giving North Korea more maneuvering room.

The first part of the strategy — the "crazy" part — is to present an image of instability and unreliability, carrying out acts that appear suicidal or counterproductive in order to sow doubt among U.S., South Korean and Japanese policymakers. This is what North Korea has been doing through the re-launch of its nuclear program — leaving observers unsure of Pyongyang's motivations or the actual status of its nuclear capabilities.

The "fearsome" part is somewhat fulfilled by North Korea's nuclear admissions, but it also requires Pyongyang to again raise the specter of a long-range missile program. If Washington continues to play hard-to-get, then it is likely that North Korea will attempt another satellite launch on a Taepodong missile, reminding its neighbors and the United States that it has the ability to deliver the nuclear weapons they suspect North Korea possesses.

The "cripple" aspect means projecting an image of weakness, something the United Nations and other international agencies do for Pyongyang. North Korea again faces a food shortage, and the number of defectors to South Korea is growing at a record pace.

With all of these elements put together, Pyongyang is portraying itself as a nation on the verge on internal collapse — a collapse that might have unpredictable and dire consequences not only for its neighbors but also for the United States. Thus, it is in the best interests of all involved not only to refrain from intentionally accelerating the collapse of the North Korean regime but to help prevent it in the first place.

Given the current policies of Beijing and Moscow, North Korea feels compelled to take this course now — playing off its potentially threatening position to squeeze concessions and time out of Washington, Seoul and Tokyo. Meanwhile, Washington continues to call Pyongyang's bluff. U.S. officials know the regime is not suicidal and therefore is extremely unlikely to attack South Korea, Japan or the United States. So Washington can wait.

But for Pyongyang, even if it cannot get Washington back to the negotiating table, it can win a consolation prize: deepening the policy differences among Seoul, Tokyo and Washington, and potentially convincing Beijing or Moscow of the importance of once more supporting Pyongyang. This gives North Korea more leverage in dealing with each nation individually and weakens any joint policies among the three.

Controlling Talks Through the Threat of Withdrawal
Jan. 10, 2003

The North Korean government announced Jan. 10 that it is withdrawing from the Nuclear Non-Proliferation Treaty (NPT). Pyongyang said it would not readmit officials from the International Atomic Energy Agency, and made it clear that the only way to resolve the current standoff is through direct bilateral negotiations with Washington.

This is not the first time Pyongyang has threatened to withdraw from the NPT. It made a similar threat in 1993, and the subsequent negotiations with Washington eventually led to the signing of the so-called Agreed Framework, in which North Korea agreed to abandon its nuclear program in return for fuel supplies and foreign-built light water nuclear reactors.

Pyongyang's new threat comes just days after U.S. officials indicated that the Bush administration was willing to discuss the nuclear standoff with North Korea, and the threat was made at the same time that North Korean envoys met with New Mexico Gov. Bill Richardson. The governor had negotiated with Pyongyang when he was the U.S. ambassador to the United Nations during the Clinton administration.

Pyongyang feels confident that its threatening tactics — along with pressure from South Korea and Japan — are drawing the United

States nearer to the bargaining table, and thus it wants to raise the stakes in order to take control of the agenda. But at its core, North Korea's tiered brinksmanship lays the groundwork for Pyongyang to gain concessions without having to truly make any itself.

The North Korean regime recently announced that it has a uranium-based nuclear program and is taking steps to restart its plutonium-based nuclear program. Now it has threatened to withdraw from the NPT. These are all chips that Pyongyang is willing to trade in return for diplomatic and economic concessions from Washington. And if the United States should agree, all North Korea loses are things that sprang into existence only in the past few months. Pyongyang will have, in essence, traded nothing.

Fear of Flying: North Korea's Economic Reforms
Feb. 15, 2003

According to the South China Morning Post, Kim Jong Il, chairman of the Workers' Party of Korea, took an 80-member entourage to China in January. Chinese Premier Zhu Rongji accompanied Kim during his four-day visit to Shanghai, where Kim toured the Shanghai Stock Exchange and a Buick plant co-owned by General Motors. As reported by Chosun Ilbo, Kim Jong Il remarked, "The state of Shanghai's development is proof that the policy of reform and opening-up adopted by the Chinese Communist Party is correct."

South Korean Foreign Affairs and Trade Minister Lee Joung Binn suggested Jan. 29 that the visit presaged economic change in the North. Speculation spread that North Korea would look to China as a model for economic development.

No doubt North Korea would like to bring its centrally planned economy out of the doldrums. North Korea's New Year Joint Editorial, printed in RoDong Sinmun, Chosoninmingun and Chongnyonchonwi, stated, "Refashioning the national economy is now a master key to economic projects and is an urgent task which cannot be delayed." From 1997 to 1999, North Korea sent more than 200 officials to numerous countries — including China — for economic training. For Pyongyang, however, following China's development strategy is impractical and unrealistic.

When China began to liberalize its economy in 1978, Shanghai enjoyed a number of advantages. Among these were the existence of eager investors, including many overseas Chinese; a massive building boom fueled in part by government resources dedicated to the improvement of its infrastructure; and trade. Shanghai is a port city, adjacent to the bustling shipping routes of the East China Sea. It has long served as an entrepot between China, Taiwan, Japan, Korea and Southeast Asia. These factors were crucial to the city's growth, which averaged 9.3 percent annually from 1979 to 1996, according to Sheinet.

North Korea has none of these advantages. Its territory is mountainous, cold, and infertile. With an economy based on Kim Il Sung's concept of juche, or self-reliance, Pyongyang has refused most economic interaction with other nations. Although North Korea has accepted international aid in recent years, largely due to prolonged famine and drought, the government has been loath to engage in trade with non-communist nations. The result is one of the world's most isolated and controlled economies. North Korea does have some port facilities, but political uncertainty and official inconsistencies serve as a deterrent to investors. The port of Nampo closed its docks to South Korean ships in December 2000 without explanation. Poor infrastructure also will undermine North Korean attempts to move ahead. Talk of connecting railways between Russia, South Korea and North Korea has been in the news. North Korea's railroad system, however, operates on a single line, whose tracks were laid during Japanese occupation, from 1910 to 1945.

Circumstances have conspired to undermine North Korea's intentions of going it alone. The collapse of the Soviet Union put an end to Soviet subsidies and trade with the Eastern Bloc. Floods and drought devastated agriculture, a sector that accounted for almost 30 percent of GNP in 1996, according to the U.S. Department of State. Famine and deprivation have forced the regime to reassess. Indeed, articles surface regularly now in various publications to assure citizens that the country will undertake "self-styled" reforms.

There is much to do. But North Korea cannot look to its former allies for further aid; Russia lacks the funds and China is currently wrapped up in its own economic reform. South Korea is North Korea's primary source of outside income. November 2000 figures from the Unification Ministry indicate the total volume of inter-Korean trade during November was $34 million, increasing 40 percent from $24 million the previous year. Kim Jong Il, however, will not allow the relationship with Seoul to threaten the regime's unity.

Therein lies the crux of the problem. The country does not have the means or capability to go it alone, but it is unwilling to relinquish enough control to allow effective economic reform. Having watched both Russia and China wrestle with reform, Pyongyang is aware of the potential for failure — or, even worse, the loss of political control.

This fear explains the regime's contradictory statements and actions. So, although recent consultations with China and an upcoming visit by Kim Jong Il to Russia in April indicate that Pyongyang probably wants to pursue similar reforms, the regime denies this is the case. The Chosun Shinbo, an online newspaper associated with pro-Pyongyang Koreans in Japan, denied that North Korea intended to model its reforms after China's. As reported by Dong-A Ilbo, the publication said that Kim felt Shanghai "would only serve as a rough guide in the development of North Korea's future policy."

China's ability to pursue reform appeals to North Korea. But factional fighting in Beijing and popular challenges to party control frighten Pyongyang. North Korea is unwilling to place its control at risk. Investors might overlook the tight controls and bureaucracy in North Korea if the state had some sort of economic incentive, such as natural resources. But, unlike China, North Korea has little to offer and won't allow the type of opening needed to bring in money.

Peace Treaty or Nuclear State?
April 18, 2003

A North Korean Foreign Ministry spokesman said April 18 that Pyongyang is "successfully reprocessing more than 8,000 spent fuel rods at the final phase ... after resuming our nuclear activities from December last year." The statement, carried by the official (North) Korean Central News Agency, also touched on the Iraq war, saying the lesson learned was that to prevent war and preserve national sovereignty, "it is necessary to have a powerful physical deterrent force only."

The comments come days before North Korean and U.S. officials are set to meet in China to resume long-stalled talks on North Korea's nuclear program. Pyongyang's apparent warning is an early signal of its bargaining position during the talks. North Korea's leadership has laid out two paths that can guarantee its security: a formal peace treaty with the United States or the formal declaration of North Korea's nuclear status. The regime in Pyongyang hopes that the latter choice is so shocking — not only to the United States but also to China, South Korea, Japan, Russia and others — that Washington will have no choice but to accede to the former.

Pyongyang's top priority in next week's nuclear talks with the United States is to sign a formal peace treaty with Washington and to do away with the 1953 Armistice Agreement. North Korea's top leadership feels constrained by the Armistice Agreement as well as by the ever-present threat of U.S. military force, and believes it cannot both retain political power and expand its economic policies significantly without first removing the threat of war on the Korean Peninsula. Barring a formal peace accord, Pyongyang would settle for a more temporal nonaggression treaty, but is unconvinced of the long-term stability of such a document.

North Korea itself carefully orchestrated the current nuclear crisis with Washington and is intent on maintaining control over the pace and scope of negotiations. Thus the meeting in Beijing is not a capitulation by Pyongyang out of fear of the United States following the Iraq war, but a carefully timed concession designed to engage Washington at a time when the U.S. military is not yet fully rested from the Iraq war and when Washington is less likely to seek a military confrontation in a different theater of battle.

Pyongyang is concerned by the U.S. military's swift capture of Baghdad and the apparent ease with which U.S. forces ultimately conquered Iraq. But the lesson learned by North Korea's leadership is not that Pyongyang should roll over and accede to whatever Washington wants. Rather, Pyongyang believes that a powerful deterrent — nuclear weapons — will serve to keep Washington from stepping over the DMZ.

According to sources familiar with the North Korean leadership, Pyongyang's assessment of the Iraq war battle plan — sending in ground forces simultaneously with the air campaign — signaled Washington's belief that Baghdad in fact possessed no deployable weapons of mass destruction. Otherwise, the U.S. military would have withheld troops until it was sure the air campaign had effectively removed the threat of chemical and biological weapons.

The conclusion in Pyongyang, the source notes, is that there are only two paths to peace and security in Korea. One is through negotiations to sign a formal peace treaty or at least a nonaggression treaty; the latter is less desirable because there is little assurance Washington will keep its word — and the international community proved impotent in preventing the U.S.-led invasion of Iraq. The other alternative is the formal declaration of North Korea as a nuclear state.

Pyongyang is well aware of the ramifications of such a move. It could easily trigger the nuclearization of the Japanese and South Korean militaries and raise the ire of China and Russia. But North Korea's strategic planners see some benefits from a nuclear Japan and South Korea, as they would render moot the U.S. nuclear umbrella in the region. And since North Korea already is facing off against a nuclear United States, what difference does it make if South Korea and Japan have the bomb?

The fear of a nuclear domino effect in Northeast Asia — even more than the fear of a nuclear-armed North Korea — is precisely the bargaining chip Pyongyang plans to employ during talks with the United States. And as U.S. military and intelligence assessments already hold that North Korea has two or three nuclear devices, in addition to stocks of chemical and biological weapons, the United States will be unlikely to launch a pre-emptive strike against North Korea, and have little choice but to negotiate.

How Washington will react to such a threat from the North remains to be seen, but China's sudden burst of involvement in the nuclear standoff suggests Beijing is well aware of Pyongyang's negotiating tactic and is itself interested in pre-empting the nuclearization of the rest of Northeast Asia, since that would seriously undermine China's physical and economic security.

Cabinet Shuffle Hints at the True Foreign Policy Goal
Sept. 6, 2003

The North Korean regime has reshuffled its Cabinet — appointing Pak Pong Ju, former minister of chemical industry, as the new prime minister. The change follows the recent resumption of nuclear talks between the United States and North Korea, and comes as Washington is making signs that it is ready for a compromise to end the nuclear crisis.

At the same time, choreographed crowds of cheering North Koreans gathered in Pyongyang to support the government's policy of strong national defense, amid its warnings of confrontation due to the "hostile policy" of the United States. Yet this show is more rhetoric and negotiating strategy than reality; Pyongyang's true intent is seen in the Cabinet change, which reflects a continuation of its willingness to experiment with market policies — a key reason Pyongyang wants to finalize a non-aggression pact with Washington.

Though Cabinet positions in North Korea are to some extent symbolic, Pak's promotion is part of a broader shift that saw several other technocrats being brought into the Cabinet as well. For North Korea, the 2003 nuclear crisis — which was planned from the earliest moments of the Bush presidency — is a complex means of gaining a security guarantee from the United States. But even this guarantee isn't the end; the North Korean regime is ready for a careful program of market reforms that will help build North Korea's economic and technological strength, freeing Pyongyang from its traditional reliance on its neighbors.

Pak's appointment as prime minister is a step toward this end. The official, who formerly was in charge of one of North Korea's key industries, is close to North Korean leader Kim Jong Il, whom he often accompanies on trips. Pak is also an economic reformer of sorts, traveling to neighboring states as part of economic delegations and investigating and studying foreign market examples and experiences.

Pak is joined by several other new or returning Cabinet members who have either a bent toward new market experiments or have shown very close devotion to Kim Jong Il. Among the former are State Planning Chairman Kim Kwang Rin, who is also close to Kim Jong Il; Mining Minister Ri Kwang Num; Minister of Metals and Machine Building Kim Sung Hyon; Minister of Power and Coal Ju Tong Il; Electronics Minister O Su Yong; Telecommunications Minister Ri Kum Bom; and Pak's replacement at the Chemical Ministry, Ri Mu Yong.

According to sources in Russia's foreign intelligence service and Foreign Ministry, these officials all have at least moderate leanings toward more market reforms, with several prominent technocrats among them. Rounding out the new Cabinet are several career bureaucrats, including Vice Prime Ministers Kwak Pom Gi and Jon Sung Hun and Railways Minister Kim Yong Sam. Two other officials, People's Security Minister Choe Ryong Su and Vice Prime Minister Ro Tu Chol, are both considered "conservatives" or "hardliners" by

Russian sources, but are also known to be strongly devoted to Kim Jong Il and will follow where he leads.

The remaining Cabinet members, Foreign Minister Paek Num Sun and Trade Minister Ri Yong Son, are both good negotiators, bright and pragmatic — qualities Pyongyang will need as it starts to re-engage foreign nations and businesses amid the carefully planned economic changes.

This is what both the Cabinet changes and the nuclear negotiations are really about — North Korea's economic independence. Despite decades of teaching a Juche "self-reliance" philosophy, North Korea long has relied upon China and Russia for support, as well as — ironically — South Korea, Japan and even the United States for economic aid. But this always placed North Korea at a disadvantage, and Kim Jong Il has slowly but steadily worked toward developing a new economic model for the country, seeking to break it free from the political constraints of its sustainers.

This is not to say that Pyongyang will suddenly throw open its doors to Western business upon the completion of negotiations over the nuclear crisis. The careful planning of the crisis itself is evidence of North Korea's nearly paranoid concern that reforms can quickly lead to destabilization — particularly at the instigating hand of a hostile foreign power. Pyongyang, which has watched Russia's economic failures and China's economic opening and reform, does not necessarily want to emulate any of their programs to the letter.

Pyongyang daily grows more desperate to strengthen its economy — the foundation of a strong defense — from the inside. But years of focusing on defense at the expense of economic strength are hard to overcome, and whatever processes Pyongyang puts in place will be tempered by periodic reversals, half measures and overly conservative steps as the regime seeks to redefine decades of economically self-destructive policies without throwing society into chaos and opening the way for regime collapse.

An Exercise in Scripted Diplomacy
Jan. 14, 2005

North Korea's official Korean Central News Agency (KCNA), in a report issued Jan. 14, said Pyongyang "would not stand against the U.S., but respect and treat it as a friend unless the latter slanders the former's system and interferes in its internal affairs." The comments follow a visit by a U.S. congressional delegation to Pyongyang, where — according to KCNA — the U.S. congressmen assured the North Korean leadership that the United States has no intention of overthrowing the government of Kim Jong Il. KCNA noted that if the United States truly had no intention and took no action to overthrow the North Korean government, Pyongyang would work to find a solution to the ongoing nuclear crisis and other issues.

The comments from North Korea on establishing friendship with the United States, while somewhat unusual in wording, are not unexpected. North Korea always has intended for the nuclear crisis, begun in late 2002, to end in the formation of diplomatic relations with the United States. When North Korea walked out of the six-party talks before the U.S. presidential elections in 2004, Pyongyang intended to restart negotiations after the U.S. inauguration, regardless of whether George W. Bush or John Kerry won the vote. It is now laying the groundwork for that.

Pyongyang's negotiating tactics often seem inexplicable to U.S. negotiators and policy formulators. North Korean negotiators will leave meetings no matter what is being discussed or how much progress appears to have been made — simply because the tactic has been pre-scripted. Perhaps even more perplexing to foreign negotiators is Pyongyang's insistence on negotiating through threats. The idea that a threat to launch nuclear war will make your opponent want to establish friendly ties with you often seems like a counterproductive tactic, at the very least.

But this is indeed how North Korea negotiates. The 2003 nuclear crisis was a carefully planned attempt by Pyongyang to threaten

Washington into signing an official peace treaty to replace the 1953 armistice that ended the Korean War. Pyongyang began planning the crisis, including the timing of threats and concessions, even before the 9/11 attacks against the United States. The problem was, once the plans were laid out, Pyongyang did not shift tactics to adjust to the new U.S. outlook, but instead tried to run through with its business-as-usual aggressive diplomacy. When Washington failed to respond to Pyongyang's threats, the North's leadership was slow to reshape its tactics, and the crisis lingered well beyond the intended mid-2003 completion date.

North Korea has, to some extent, reshaped its negotiating policies and started playing on the differing desires of Seoul, Tokyo, Beijing and Washington. Ultimately, however, Pyongyang's intent — and need — is to deal with the United States, which is the signatory to the armistice, not South Korea or Japan. Underlying this desire for a peace accord and diplomatic relations with Washington is economics.

It is not a coincidence that Kim's first two public appearances of 2005 were at the Pukjung Machine complex and the September General Iron Enterprise complex — backbones of North Korea's heavy industry. Kim is seeking to reshape the North Korean economy but is convinced that any opening also could create an opportunity for the United States to undermine the social structure in North Korea and lay the groundwork for social instability and the collapse of the government. He also fears that foreign investors from Europe and Asia will shy away from the country if North Korean/U.S. relations are seen as hostile, and he hopes that investors would flood in should diplomatic ties be established.

That is North Korea's ultimate goal — diplomatic ties with the United States. Although Pyongyang would certainly accept a peace accord or security guarantee, those are short-term solutions. For the Kim regime to survive, North Korea must break out of the U.S. containment box — and it cannot do that by following the Libyan model; North Korea has no valuable resources that make it an important and useful player on the world stage. From Pyongyang's viewpoint, anything shy of formal diplomatic relations would not prevent

Washington from trying to undermine the regime and destabilize the country.

Pyongyang, while often slow in adjusting its own plans, does keep a keen eye on the world, and it is offering an opening for talks right around the U.S. presidential inauguration to ensure North Korea is on the agenda for the early part of the second Bush term. But the timing also coincides with the Iraqi elections, which are unlikely to look like the glorious victory for democracy that some in Washington might have envisioned. Pyongyang is holding out the hope to Washington that the U.S. government can look good by solving the North Korean nuclear crisis, thus diverting some of the negative attention away from the Iraqi situation.

And there are indications from Washington that it is preparing to put the nuclear crisis behind it, particularly if North Korea is willing to modify its demands. In the end, an anticlimactic resolution is the most likely, with neither side holding to its most extreme positions, but little actually being resolved aside from returning to the 2002 status quo. The next move is Washington's.

North Korea's Nuclear Declaration
Feb. 10, 2005

North Korea's Foreign Ministry has made the first official admission of the country's manufacture of nuclear weapons. In a statement directed at the United States on Feb. 10, the ministry said North Korea "had already taken the resolute action of pulling out of the NPT [Nuclear Nonproliferation Treaty] and has manufactured nukes for self-defense to cope with the Bush administration's ever more undisguised policy to isolate and stifle the DPRK." Before this point, Pyongyang has always played coy regarding its nuclear weapons program, preferring to claim the "right" to weapons or simply referring to deterrents and the ability to turn various cities into seas of fire.

Washington long has argued that North Korea has nuclear weapons — with most estimates ranging from three to seven bombs — so Pyongyang's announcement is more a question of motive and timing than a revelation. In addition, it is a rhetorical, rather than substantive, shift, as Pyongyang has yet to carry out a nuclear test; therefore the actual knowledge of the North's true nuclear capability remains unchanged. So why make the announcement, and why now?

The timing is particularly interesting. It comes on the first day of the Lunar New Year, the second most important holiday in the Koreas and a time when much of Asia is on vacation. This makes reaction times slower in Asia, but the message clearly is received in the United States. The statement criticizes Washington and Tokyo but makes no mention of Seoul — perhaps a nod to the recently released South Korean defense white paper that no longer uses the term "main enemy" to describe North Korea.

North Korea has just undertaken a series of rallies and meetings extolling Kim Jong Il's Songun policies, and Kim's birthday — an important occasion in the North — is less than a week away. There have been rumors in the past couple of months of serious cracks in the North Korean regime, matched by conflicting rumors that Kim is preparing the way for another dynastic succession and is about to start raising one of his sons to a much higher status in the country.

In addition, Pyongyang has laid out hints that it is ready for dialogue with the United States and waited to see how Washington would address Pyongyang in Bush's second term. The response was, apparently, unsatisfactory. Pyongyang was anything but reassured by U.S. Secretary of State Condoleezza Rice's "outpost of tyranny" remarks because they lumped North Korea in with Zimbabwe in the rankings of U.S. foreign policy interests and indicated Washington's goal for North Korea remained — and was perhaps even more so now — all about regime change.

Pyongyang's new message of nuclear weapons possession was matched with calls for dialogue and a desire to de-nuclearize the Korean Peninsula. In reality, Pyongyang still wants to negotiate; it still wants a peace accord and diplomatic relations with the United

YONGBYON NUCLEAR FACILITY

DIGITALGLOBE
Copyright STRATFOR 2011   www.STRATFOR.com

States — but only because that is considered an assurance that Washington will not try to topple the regime. That belief is fading, however, as Pyongyang has watched Ukrainian elections and realizes that diplomatic ties have little to do with noninterference in regime transitions. Thus, from Pyongyang's perspective, the only surety of security is through military power — which is, not coincidentally, the very essence of Kim's Songun politics.

A source close to the North Korean regime says that although Pyongyang wants dialogue, it will not participate if there is no hope for a change of U.S. position. Pyongyang's statement is a final call for talks — a narrow "window" of opportunity — and if the talks are rejected, Pyongyang has basically signaled it will be unable to go back from its development and possession of nuclear weapons. This is not a new threat — Pyongyang used a similar negotiating ploy in 2003 — but the warning of a closing window is somewhat ominous since it hints at a nuclear test, which is an undeniable verification of North Korean nuclear capability.

And while public reactions are fairly muted — after all, North Korea always negotiates through brinkmanship — there are less open concerns that North Korea might not be bluffing, and that could lead to a reshaping of the security environment in Northeast Asia if Japan and South Korea, and possibly even Taiwan, fall like dominoes into the international nuclear club. Already, sources in the Russian Ministry of Defense say Moscow has quietly put the Pacific Fleet and Rocket Forces on high alert to prevent any U.S. incursion into Russian airspace should the rhetoric degrade into action.

The next move is Washington's. North Korea has set a very clear choice for the U.S. administration: engage in a productive dialogue with Pyongyang directly or accept the reality of a nuclear-armed North Korea — and the collapse of U.S. nonproliferation actions. North Korea is a cautious and careful planner, and a keen observer of global events, and while there is certainly a particular lens through which the nation's leaders and planners view things, their motivation is clear.

With the 60th anniversary of the founding of the Workers' Party of Korea approaching this year, Pyongyang intends to be free from the U.S. box, whether through dialogue or nuclear tests — and it is banking on Washington either seeking to avoid the latter or reshape Northeast Asia into a region where all nations are nuclear-armed, thus reducing the significance of Washington's nuclear umbrella — and influence.

Tertiary Powers and the Nuclear Gambit
Feb. 17, 2005

Last week, North Korea announced it had nuclear devices. It should be made clear that Pyongyang did not claim to have deliverable nuclear weapons — those small and robust enough to be fitted on an aircraft or missile and delivered to the target — but that fine point seemed unimportant compared to the claim that the country had gone nuclear. The Iranians also seem eager to develop nuclear weapons or, to be more precise, seem eager to establish that they are capable of developing nuclear weapons and willing to do so.

Assuming that neither nation is irrational — and there is nothing we can see in either's behavior, as opposed to statements, that they are — there is a mystery to solve. First, why would they be so eager to develop nuclear weapons, and why would they be so casual in letting the world know that they are either trying to develop or already have such weapons? More generally stated, what is the value of nuclear weapons or the pursuit thereof for tertiary powers?

The obvious use of nuclear weapons is to attack other countries. The leaders of North Korea and Iran know, of course, that the actual use of the very small number of weapons they might have or acquire would result in some country, probably the United States, delivering an overwhelming counterstrike that would devastate their states — and kill most of the leadership. Therefore, it is extraordinarily difficult to imagine circumstances in which either country would initiate the use of nuclear weapons. The obvious reason, therefore, cannot be the correct reason. Nuclear-armed tertiary powers can hurt other countries badly, but only at the cost of suicide — or, to be more precise, the probability of suicide is sufficiently high to deter action.

Another reason might simply be to deter conventional attack. The United States, outgunned by Soviet forces in Central Europe during the Cold War, used the threat of nuclear strike to deter the Soviets from attacking. It seemed to have worked, at least in the sense that the Soviets never invaded Germany. But the fact is that there might have been other reasons. The Soviets had tremendous logistical problems they never really solved that made a massive armored thrust into Germany difficult to sustain beyond the initial strike. They might never have felt they could have successfully carried out such a maneuver, even absent U.S. nuclear weapons.

But there is another case that further complicates the idea that nuclear weapons deter conventional attack. In 1973, the Egyptians and Syrians attacked Israel — knowing the Israelis had a substantial nuclear capability. Now, it might have been that they did not expect to destroy Israel, but only to conduct limited operations. The Egyptians and Syrians therefore might have assumed the Israelis would not use nuclear weapons in any case unless their existence was threatened.

The problem was that (a) the Egyptians and Syrians could not know whether this was Israeli doctrine and (b) they did not know whether the Israelis would perceive the attack as limited or as a mortal threat to their own existence. Indeed, the Israelis appear to have been contemplating a nuclear strike during the first 24 hours of the war, when their perception was that Israel's existence was indeed in peril from Syrian successes in the Golan Heights. Therefore, this was a case in which two non-nuclear powers attacked a nuclear power, using conventional forces. Nuclear weapons did not deter them.

Consider Vietnam and Afghanistan. In both cases, superpowers were engaged in multi-year counterinsurgencies that they were losing — or, at the least, not winning. Both powers had thousands of nuclear weapons. Each chose to lose the counterinsurgency, despite substantial political costs, rather than resort to using nuclear weapons. Indeed, in neither case would it appear that the use of nuclear weapons was seriously contemplated.

Consider also the case of the Korean War. North Korea attacked South Korea, the Chinese intervened in the war, and the Soviet Union, not yet a nuclear power in the sense of being able to deliver a nuclear device to the continental United States, provided substantial political and logistical support — despite the fact that the United States could deliver at least limited nuclear strikes to all three countries at the outset of the war.

And finally, consider the Kargil affair in 1999, when two nuclear powers — India and Pakistan — fought each other in a conventional war. Despite global tremors that a nuclear event was at hand, the range of both countries' missiles and mutually assured destruction did, indeed, act as a deterrent. This holds despite the fact that a nuclear strike might have definitively solved the conflict in favor of Pakistan, since India conducted few significant counterstrikes outside the Kashmir region.

From these cases, we can extract the following empirical principles:

- The possession of a very small number of nuclear weapons — one or two — makes their use irrational. In a context in which others possess greater numbers of nuclear weapons, their use would lead to annihilation of the initiator's country and leadership.

- Possession of large numbers of nuclear weapons will not, by itself, deter a conventional attack by non-nuclear powers, particularly if they are seeking political outcomes other than the annihilation of the target country. However, since outcomes and perceived outcomes are beyond the control of the attacker at times, even the threat of enemy misperception will not deter attack. Even complete asymmetry, where only one power has nuclear weapons and no other powers at all possess them in any meaningful way, does not shift the calculus of attackers substantially.

- The possession of extremely large numbers of nuclear weapons does not prevent defeat in war. Indeed, major nuclear powers accept defeat by minor non-nuclear powers, particularly in counterinsurgency situations.

The possibility of mutually assured destruction in a nuclear conflict does not eliminate the possibility of conventional warfare involving two primary actors.

In looking at the last 60 years, the only case in which nuclear weapons were used was as the logical conclusion of an extensive counter-population bombing campaign that was already under way, at the conclusion of a multi-year war that had evolved into total war — meaning that no outcome except total annihilation of the enemy regime was conceivable. Moreover, these weapons were used when the target was incapable of retaliation and no other power possessed nuclear weapons.

Nuclear weapons, therefore, appear to have very few uses. It is not an accident, from our standpoint, that even substantial proliferation to regimes that do not seem to be self-restrained — such as Maoist China — did not result in the use of nuclear weapons. One theory for this is that possession of these weapons induces a certain sobriety that inevitably leads to self-restraint. This might be true, but there are too many nuclear or near-nuclear powers that could have used the devices in specific circumstances and yet chose not to.

The problem of nuclear weapons is that their direct use does not appear to be viewed as setting the stage for satisfactory political outcomes. Consider the case of Israel in 1973. While battlefield nuclear weapons (very small-yield weapons that can be surgically targeted at enemy units without inflicting massive casualties on friendly forces) might be useful, there are usually alternatives. Moreover, the technical sophistication needed to develop and use these weapons is well beyond the reach of entry-level nuclear players.

More basic nuclear weapons — city-killers — have limited uses. In 1973, the destruction of Damascus and Cairo would not necessarily have changed the equation on the battlefield. Indeed, with their capitals destroyed, the troops on the ground might have had greater motivation to battle the Israelis. Similarly, the failure to use nuclear weapons in Vietnam or Afghanistan is easily explained: There were no targets that required nuclear weapons — and their use might have produced defiance rather than capitulation by the enemy forces.

Why, then, would North Korea or Iran be seeking nuclear weapons? They are expensive to build, vulnerable to destruction before they are detonated, and not clearly useful to achieve any meaningful end. The usual explanation for nuclear weapons programs is regime preservation, but the problem is that, as we have seen, regime change frequently comes from sudden, internal collapse. Moreover, it is simply not clear that the possession of nuclear weapons will deter external aggression. If dozens or even hundreds of sophisticated devices owned by Israel did not deter Egypt or Syria, why would one or two missiles deter the United States — particularly when neither Pyongyang nor Tehran has the ability to deliver weapons to the U.S. mainland?

There is always the lunatic theory, which is that Iran and North Korea are both governed by people who are either insane or whose value system is so extreme that the annihilation of their country by counterstrikes is no deterrent. That is a useful way not to think about the problem. Neither the Iranians nor North Koreans have ever engaged in irrational foreign activity. Quite the contrary, most of their behavior is carefully calculated and, to a great extent, risk-averse. This is to be distinguished from their rhetoric, which does at times — particularly in the case of North Korea — appear to be completely off-the-wall.

The North Koreans and Iranians both project a carefully honed image of irrationality — but with a very rational purpose. When playing poker, appearing to be irrational and unpredictable causes other players to try to avoid your moves, and thus increases your leverage. You are given room to maneuver, whereas if every bet you made was predictable, the other players would be all over you. Appearing to be slightly cracked is one of the keys to profitable poker.

This tactic is particularly cogent in the post-9/11 era, since fears of nuclear technology sales to non-state actors such as al Qaeda can further increase the leverage of tertiary powers.

Both Iran and North Korea project an external image of being slightly cracked. If you focus on the image rather than the reality, then obviously, you will want to deal very carefully with each of them. One wrong step on your part might trigger unpleasant results. How unpleasant the results might be matters a great deal. If you are dealing with a player without many chips, it doesn't matter how crazy he is.

Therefore, Iran and North Korea need to have more chips available. Craziness and a large stack of chips are formidable weapons. Neither country is inherently powerful — North Korea should have about as much influence as, say, Chad. But if you are trying to carve out freedom of maneuver for yourself, you need to get more chips on the table.

That is the value of a few nuclear weapons — or some nearly completed nuclear weapons. When combined with a reputation for irrational behavior, they shift the behavior of others toward you. Since you are irrational, any aggressive move could trigger unpleasant consequences — and if you have or may have nuclear weapons, the consequences could be horrifying.

There are countries that want things from North Korea or Iran, but no one wants these things enough to trigger a nuclear reaction from either. Since both countries are seen as dangerous, potentially suicidal or quite mad, these demands are not made as forcefully as might otherwise be the case. "Let the lunatics do what they want" becomes the standard view. Suddenly, regime preservation is at hand.

The key to this maneuver is to never be critical to any others' strategy or to be so convincingly mad that no one would risk attacking you. Obviously, the more something is needed, the more risks you will take. Therefore, it is essential for North Korea or Iran to avoid being critical to the plans of any other countries, and to appear sufficiently unpredictable so as to deter external pressure.

Nuclear weapons, therefore, are useful primarily in the context of small countries that sense threats to their regimes. They craft, using materials at hand, an image of irrationality — which becomes valuable only when they also possess military power of sufficient size as to deter pressure. The cheapest path here is nuclear power. Using the combination of irrational behavior and nuclear weapons, North Korea has become the focus of five great powers, treating Pyongyang as an equal. Should Iran manage to build nuclear weapons — which we doubt other powers will permit — it also would be able to play that game. Indeed, the mere fact that the Iranians are pursuing weapons has given them leverage.

Nuclear weapons, in this context, are not to be seen as military elements but as a complement to a strategy of regime survival. For the United States and others, the proper counter is to recognize that the regime is far from irrational, and that it is less interested in being incinerated than in doing the incinerating. At that point, the advantage of the "irrational" regime dissolves, and North Korea goes back to being North Korea.

Nothing in North Korean or Iranian history indicates the slightest element of irrationality on major issues. This is simply wishful thinking on the part of Western powers that has now been turned into their nightmare. The nuclear weapons are simply part of a general posture designed as deterrent pressure. It has worked extremely well.

Economic Reform and the Nuclear Crisis
March 28, 2005

North Korean Prime Minister Pak Pong Ju returned to Pyongyang on March 27 after a six-day visit to Beijing that had been touted, at least by the Chinese, as relating to the resumption of the six-party nuclear talks. Apparently, little was accomplished on that front as Pak simply repeated the North Korean line that it is ready to resume talks when the United States changes its tone toward the regime and apologizes for referring to North Korea as "evil" and an "outpost of tyranny."

More important was the second half of Pak's visit, which included trips to Shanghai, Shenzhen and the northeastern province of Liaoning. Pak traveled to China mainly to further study China's experience with its economic reform and opening program. Pak, the current engineer of North Korea's economic opening, observed both the success (Shanghai) and the future focus (Liaoning) of China's reforms.

It is important to remember that North Korea started the 2003 nuclear crisis, now in its third year, as a way of facilitating economic experiments. Although it might seem counterintuitive at first, the North Korean regime is extremely concerned about the social and political instability that reforms can engender. It wants to leave little or no room for other countries — such as the United States — to exploit those instabilities and bring down the regime.

Pak has been to China before, as part of North Korean leader Kim Jong Il's entourage to China in 2004. He also visited South Korea in 2002 as minister of chemical industry. Pak, whose rise has been meteoric by North Korean standards, started as a manager at a foodstuffs factory in North Pyongan province before being named an alternate member of the Workers' Party of Korea (WPK) Central Committee in 1980.

In 1983 he was appointed chief secretary of the Namhung Youth Chemical complex, and a decade later was the deputy director of the WPK Light Industry Department. He became deputy director of the WPK Economic Policy Inspection Department in 1994. With the death of Kim Il Sung, Pak found himself among the official state funeral committee members. In 1998, he was named a deputy in the 10th Supreme People's Assembly, and named minister of chemical industry. In April 2002, he was among those awarded the Order of Kim Il Sung, one of the highest honors in North Korea. In September 2003, he was named prime minister of North Korea.

Pak apparently is a self-made man — rather than the son of an elite WPK or military member — a fact that signals his drive but also offers insight into his potential capabilities to oversee the economy as prime minister. He is an economic "reformer," but that does not mean he opposes the North Korean Songun "Army First" policy. Far from it.

Like most North Korean leaders, he is convinced that economic reform is fully effective only in nations with minimal external threat — and that the only way a country as small as North Korea can minimize the threat is to have a strong deterrent. North Korean leaders view the economic might of the United States as a direct result of its ability to ensure its own security at home and abroad.

This is the underlying justification for the North Korean nuclear program and the periodic crises, which are intended ultimately to eliminate the state of hostilities between Washington and Pyongyang — without Pyongyang showing weakness.

Playing the Nuclear Disarmament Card
March 31, 2005

A North Korean Foreign Ministry spokesman says the six-party talks on North Korea's nuclear program should be transformed into disarmament talks centered on the Korean Peninsula. The spokesman, cited by the North's official Korean Central News Agency on March 31, said the talks should provide a forum for all parties to enter the discussions on an equal footing — as North Korea is now a "full-fledged nuclear weapons state."

The announcement came less than a week after North Korean Prime Minister Pak Pong Ju visited China, where he met with President Hu Jintao and other officials and toured key economic sites in Shanghai, Shenzhen and the northeast. Pak's visit did not result in any major breakthrough announcement about restarting the six-way nuclear talks, however, and at the moment it is unclear whether Pyongyang communicated its new negotiating position to Beijing.

Since its Feb. 10 Lunar New Year announcement formally declaring the possession of nuclear weapons, North Korea has worked aggressively to retake the initiative in the nuclear talks and draw the United States into negotiations. On March 3, for example, Pyongyang announced an end to its self-imposed moratorium on ballistic missile tests, effectively implying not only that it was nuclear-armed but also that it had delivery capability.

In the midst of the threats, Pyongyang also repeatedly offered an opening to talks — if the United States changed its tone and apologized for calling Pyongyang "evil" and an "outpost of tyranny." It also continued quiet dialogue with Seoul, with a semi-official meeting of representatives of North and South Korea in Kaesong on March 30, as well as continued cooperation in the economic realm in the border city.

And China has not stopped its involvement either, sending a "goodwill delegation" to Pyongyang on March 29, headed by Ma Wen, deputy secretary of the Communist Party of China's Central Commission for Discipline Inspection.

But while China has sought to coax North Korea back into the six-party talks, Pyongyang appears to have decided to press forward with its own "security guarantee" and simultaneously exploit the dynamics of the six-party talks to reset the agenda.

The call for multilateral disarmament talks is a clear message that North Korea will negotiate away its nuclear deterrent only if it can simultaneously negotiate cuts in the U.S. military presence in South Korea and the surrounding region. This is by no means a new position for North Korea; it has frequently called for the reduction of U.S. forces in the region and as recently as January was accusing the United States of having some 1,000 nuclear warheads targeted on North Korea.

By shifting the debate from North Korean nuclear adventurism to the core balance of power in the region, Pyongyang is hoping to take advantage of the splits among the six parties — China, Russia, North Korea, South Korea, Japan and the United States — to either maneuver Washington back into discussions with a favorable outcome for the North or to maintain a North Korean deterrent while not undermining its attempts at economic experimentation.

In the latter, Pyongyang has received some positive signs, particularly from Seoul. Despite North Korea's announcement of a nuclear weapons arsenal, Seoul went ahead with economic cooperation on the Kaesong complex, even starting new electricity supplies across the border into the northern city. From Seoul's perspective, North Korea might be a threat, but if the South is ever to advance to its goal as a regional economic hub, it needs Northern participation. The South Korean government clearly understands the North's threat — but sees it as secondary to the potential for cooperation.

This is one of the unique ironies of the nuclear standoff at this time — that South Korea is perhaps the biggest cheerleader for engagement, despite (or perhaps because of) being directly under the North's guns. Pyongyang has learned to manipulate the complexity of the six-party talks quite well. Having six parties involved is more than six votes; it entails 15 individual bilateral relationships among the six nations as well, leaving plenty of room for manipulation.

Ultimately, however, the North's latest announcement indicates that Pyongyang is growing less and less convinced that Washington will re-enter talks. By positing disarmament talks — which would require the United States to change its defense posture as well — North Korea has changed the impression that this is nuclear blackmail for aid money. After all, the South continues to aid North Korea despite the nuclear threats. Instead, Pyongyang is seeking to place itself at the center of the regional balance of power question.

With Japan debating away its constitutional restraints on its military, tensions rising between China and Taiwan, between South Korea and Japan, China and Japan, and China and the United States, North Korea is reminding all that a nuclear North Korea could open the Pandora's Box of nuclear armament in Northeast Asia. This is a last offer to Washington. Should it fail, North Korea feels secure in its deterrent and its ability to continue to work with China and South Korea — in spite of the nuclear comments.

Pyongyang has hinted it intends the current nuclear crisis to be over by mid-August, whether through a negotiated settlement or the acceptance of North Korea as a nuclear state. It has delayed its

Supreme People's Assembly session, likely because it wants to reveal the successor to Kim Jong Il in an atmosphere of less ambiguity. It has accelerated studies of foreign economic experiences and has continued to tweak its own economic programs. And it is now finding a way around the very effective U.S. strategy of ignoring North Korean demands and sidelining the nuclear threat.

North Korea's survival requires international attention and the strong interest of sponsors to prop up the regime. With U.S.-Chinese and U.S.-Russian relations deteriorating, and with Seoul pursuing an "independent" foreign policy, Pyongyang sees its window of survivability opening once again. If North Korea assesses the situation accurately and plays its cards right, the United States and Japan could be left on the sidelines.

The Value of a Nuclear Program
Sept. 22, 2005

This was a week of nuclear weapons. The North Koreans seemed to promise that they would abandon their nuclear weapons program, while the Iranians made it clear that they had no intention of abandoning theirs. This confluence of events causes us to raise a fundamental question rarely addressed: Why would small nations want to spend their national treasure on developing a handful of nuclear weapons that would be difficult to deliver to a target and that could be destroyed by another country — like the United States — almost at will, if the United States chose to use their own enormously more plentiful weapons?

The answer is not as obvious as it might seem. One of the concerns normally expressed about the North Korean nuclear program is that Pyongyang might one day choose to destroy Tokyo. That is not a trivial concern, but it is not clearly a realistic one. Assume that North Korea developed four or five fission bombs. Assume also that it fired some of those weapons at Tokyo. Obviously, Tokyo would be destroyed. But what would North Korea gain? The most likely outcome — certainly one that the North Koreans would have to assess as the most likely response — would be a massive counterstrike by the United States. The intent not only would be punitive but it would also be to destroy any remaining nuclear weapons and capabilities.

In this scenario, then, Tokyo would be lost, but so would North Korea. Thus, for the original equation to work, it has to be assumed that the North Koreans are crazy or that the Iranians have reached such a level of religious intensity that the destruction of Tel Aviv would be worth the rain of destruction that would be brought against Iran by Israel's much larger nuclear capability. The standard analysis, therefore, begins with the assumption that nuclear weapons in the hands of smaller nations — particularly North Korea or Iran — are dangerous because these countries have non-rational calculations of their national interests. They are religious fanatics, ideological fanatics or simply nuts. Therefore, their possession of nuclear weapons poses a tremendous danger. The mere desire to develop nuclear weapons is a sign of instability (among anyone other than large nations who already have them, of course).

Before buying into the lunatic theory, let's consider what happened this week. North Korea, for example, took part in a six-power conference — meeting with representatives of South Korea, Japan, Russia, China and the United States. Absent nuclear weapons, North Korea has the intrinsic geopolitical weight of Ethiopia. For it to be noticed by any of these nations, except perhaps South Korea, would require a natural disaster. But here the North Koreans were, hanging with the big dogs, all because they might be in the process of developing a few small nuclear devices — the deliverability and reliability of which were completely unclear.

Iran is a much more substantial country than North Korea in every respect. It is not, however, a great power, let alone a superpower. Nevertheless, the United States is focused obsessively on Iran's capabilities, while Germany, France and Britain stand ready to mediate and deliver stern warnings. Russians send messages to the United

States via their relations with Iran, while the Chinese buy oil and happily fish in muddy waters. Iran would always have international attention, but certainly not on the order that it receives every time it rattles its nuclear development program.

The possession of a nuclear weapons development program has one obvious result: International attention is drawn to the country developing the weapon. It really doesn't matter much how well the country is doing in developing the weapon; it is only necessary that the intent be known and their ability to build the weapon uncertain. The question is, therefore, what the value is of being noticed, when one of the consequences of being noticed might be a pre-emptive nuclear strike.

There has been only one pre-emptive strike against a nuclear capability, and that in itself wasn't a nuclear strike — it was Israel's attack against Iraq's Osirak reactor in 1981. Other than that, nuclear programs have not been attacked. The reason is simple: Those who might choose to attack are loath to use nuclear weapons. It is not in their interest to break the effective taboo that has been in place since Nagasaki. A conventional strike is uncertain at best. After Iraq, countries have learned to disperse and harden their nuclear programs. Preemptive strikes, barring massive provocation or imminent threat, have simply not been practical or desirable.

The normal response by world leaders has been to find levers that are persuasive to the country developing nuclear weapons. Once you get past the "stiff diplomatic note" stage — i.e., hot air — the options are penalties and rewards.

There are usually a range of penalties, economic and political. The problem is that — as with all international sanctions — they require unanimity, at least among major powers. Since at least one power invariably finds it in its interest to circumvent the sanctions for political or economic reasons, sanctions usually turn out to be useless. Indeed, sanctions have the mild benefit of making the country involved appear to be the victim of great-power bullying. There is always some value in that.

The real benefit occurs, however, when the carrot is used. Since military action is not desired, since stern warnings embodied by U.N. resolutions don't carry as much weight as they might and since sanctions rarely work, all that is left is the carrot. At a certain point, if the United States or some other country becomes convinced that the North Koreans, for example, are really developing a bomb — and simultaneously become convinced that they might, for whatever perverse reason, use it — a game of "Let's Make a Deal" begins. Whether it is money, food, technology, politics or season tickets to the Dallas Cowboys, the discussion usually comes around to a payoff.

North Korea, which pioneered this model, learned that in order to carry this out successfully, three things were needed:

- It is imperative for the world to know North Korea has a secret program under way. A truly secret program would have no value. Therefore, it is important to permit international inspections long enough to confirm that you are building a weapon, and then to expel the inspectors in order to frighten everyone around you.

- It is vital that you adopt a political culture in which foreigners believe that the total annihilation of your country is a matter of monumental indifference to you, so long as you get to destroy part of some other country. At the very least, you must appear crazy enough to raise questions in the minds of foreign diplomats as to whether you might do something crazy.

- You must never actually do anything really crazy, like make it appear that you are about to launch a nuclear attack with your three weapons. Since you're not really good at this yet, it will take time to move the weapon, load it on a missile or plane and launch it. During that time, someone might conclude that you really have weapons and that you really have lost your mind and nuke you. Don't do anything that actually appears to make you an immediate danger — just create the impression that you are almost posing an immediate danger. It's probably best to spend 10 years almost ready to be a threat.

Now, this entire strategy rests on one key assumption: that your country is situated in a sufficiently strategic locale that great powers should care whether you have nuclear weapons or not. Otherwise, you might find yourself following the Libyan model — making all the right poker moves and not exciting anyone, because there is nothing really important within reach of your potential weapons. This might also explain why other small countries, such as Argentina and South Africa, simply gave up their pursuit of nuclear programs. In the game of nuclear poker, as in geopolitics, "place" matters.

The geographic locations of both North Korea and Iran are important, and for the past decade or so, the North Koreans have been giving a clinic on how to extract maximum value from almost having a nuclear weapon and appearing to be nuts. They have gotten money, food, technology. Most of all, they have been treated as the equal of the United States, China, Russia, Japan and South Korea. This has tremendous value domestically, in that it legitimizes the regime. It also creates a bargaining situation that not only allows Pyongyang to extract benefits but also achieves the ultimate political goal.

That goal is regime survival. With the end of the Cold War, North Korea's survival was in serious jeopardy. It had survived by being of some value to the Soviets or to the Chinese. By the early 1990s, however, North Korea no longer was of value to anyone. The probability of the regime in Pyongyang surviving appeared minimal. But developing and publicizing its nuclear program made North Korea a wild card: It was too dangerous to attack or even to undermine. Its nuclear program was in an uncertain state — and the regime, feeling threatened, might choose to go nuclear. There was, therefore, a consensus that the survival of the North Korean regime was less of a problem than its fall, which was just the consensus North Korea was after.

Iran has learned a great deal from the North Koreans. It has learned that it is extremely important for the world to know it has a nuclear program, and Tehran has been quite content to allow inspectors in — and then jerk them around after they have confirmed everyone's worst fears. The Iranians have learned to display a political culture that forces other nations to believe they are quite capable of using nuclear weapons, even at the price of national catastrophe. They have learned to be extraordinarily cautious in not crossing a line that would bring down a pre-emptive strike. It makes no sense to do what Saddam Hussein did, which was to spend a fortune on a nuclear facility that the Israelis then blew up.

The Iranians have used their nuclear program in a far more sophisticated manner than have the North Koreans. The North Koreans engaged in very skillful quid pro quos, with the only complexity being that they just about never kept their word after they got what they wanted. The Iranians are not nearly as concerned about regime survival as the North Koreans. Their regime is going to survive. Iranian leaders are concerned with a range of regional issues, the most important at this moment being Iraq.

The Iranian interest in Iraq is profound. Tehran wants to see the creation of an Iraq that, at the very least, poses no threat to Iran — and which would be, at most, an Iranian satellite. The Iranians and Americans are engaged in a dizzyingly complex game in Iraq, and Tehran needs every lever it can find. The nuclear card increases the Iranians' leverage and gives them something with which to bargain. They also managed to skillfully draw in the British, French and Germans as mediators in an effort to drive another wedge between the United States and the Europeans. They have not been fully successful at this, but so long as the ultimate threat is recourse to the U.N. Security Council — where any resolution permitting military action will be vetoed — they have channeled the process in harmless directions.

The value of a nuclear program for a small country is not that it provides a military option. It does not. The value is not even in possessing nuclear weapons, which might actually turn out to be too dangerous. The value of a nuclear program is that it exists and is known to exist. That very fact redefines its possessor's place in the international system and provides it with opportunities to extract concessions. So long as the country does not push its position in such a way that anyone is convinced of an imminent threat — or, to put it differently, so long as the line between potential threat and "ready to launch" is never crossed — great powers will sooner make concessions than take risks.

In other words, North Korea and Iran are very rationally engaged in appearing to be irrational risk-takers. It is interesting to note that, aside from its pursuit of nuclear weapons, North Korea has taken few strategic risks since the end of the Korean War, while Iran — willing to underwrite any number of covert groups — has been very careful, since the end of the Iran-Iraq war, with its own military adventures. If we forget the rhetoric, these are countries that have prudently managed risks. Possessing a program to develop nuclear weapons is, therefore, part of a prudent portfolio for managing their position in a dangerous world. It only appears to be risky. In practice, it reduces risk by limiting the threats others pose against them and by increasing the willingness of others to make concessions.

When playing poker, the cautious player always hides his caution behind a mask of recklessness. That is the prerequisite for bluffing effectively and getting people to call into full houses. The development of nuclear programs — not the weapons themselves — is a useful part of the mask of recklessness. Until, that is, someone calls the bluff, telling North Korea to go develop all the weapons it wants and that if it deploys a single one on a launcher it will be nuked. But the North Koreans are betting, as is Iran, that that is too much for the United States to push into the pot. They are probably right.

Missile-Launch Rumors and Regime Preservation
May 31, 2006

North Korean Foreign Minister Paek Nam Sun arrived in Beijing on May 30 for a weeklong visit that will include a trip to Guangdong and a meeting with Chinese Foreign Minister Li Zhaoxing. The visit comes amid heightened efforts to bring North Korea back to the six-party negotiating table. It also comes amid continued rumors of a new North Korean long-range missile launch.

In mid-May, Japanese media said Pyongyang was preparing to carry out a Taepodong-2 missile test, citing sources in China. According to the reports, North Korea had carried out a successful ground test of a new missile engine at the Musudan-ri facility in northeastern North Korea, and a 35-meter (about 38 yards) missile body had been delivered to the site. The Taepodong-2 has an estimated range of 6,000 kilometers (about 3,728 miles), making it capable of reaching Guam and parts of Alaska.

Missile Tests and Unintended Consequences

While South Korea played down the initial reports, and no launch has thus far occurred, North Korea has continued to cultivate the sense of uncertainty surrounding its missile development. While the most recent satellite photos do not appear to show any new activity at the Musudan-ri facility, Pyongyang has made a career of showing hints of activity or misleading movements to passing satellites to manipulate international impressions. Furthermore, in March 2005, as part of its negotiating tactics to try to threaten the United States and other members of the six-party talks into granting new concessions, North Korea declared it was no longer bound by its self-imposed moratorium on testing long-range ballistic missiles. North Korea voluntarily imposed that ban on itself in 1999, following the 1998 test of a Taepodong-1 missile from the Musudan-ri launch facility.

The 1998 test was intended to place a satellite into orbit, demonstrating North Korea's technical prowess despite international isolation as Kim Jong Il formally took the reins of power four years after the death of his father, Kim Il Sung. The Kwangmyongsong No. 1 satellite, of which North Korea later released photos, was a very primitive system, similar in configuration to early Chinese satellites.

NORTH KOREAN MUSUDAN-RI MISSLE LAUNCH FACILITY, MAY 24, 2006

Taepodong missile assembly facility

Launch facility/gantry

Missile engine testing facility

Copyright STRATFOR 2011

DIGITALGLOBE

www.STRATFOR.com

There was an apparent failure on the third stage of the Taepodong-1, however, and the satellite never went into its proper orbit. Despite this, Pyongyang touted the success of the launch, even claiming it could receive the Morse code broadcast of the "Song of General Kim Il Sung" and the "Song of General Kim Jong Il" from the satellite.

The launch did raise North Korea's international status, but not exactly in the way Pyongyang predicted. Rather than shock people into recognizing North Korea's advances and into breaking down Pyongyang's isolation, the launch created tremendous concern in Japan and contributed to Tokyo's efforts to reshape the Japanese Self-Defense Forces' mission and capabilities. Ultimately, Tokyo joined the effort to create a U.S. anti-missile defense system and began a series of domestic spy satellite launches, initially geared toward North Korea but with a long-term focus on China.

The 1998 launch, coupled with the latent North Korean nuclear crisis, nearly invited air strikes from the United States. North Korea defused the tensions with its missile moratorium and, ultimately, with a rapid diplomatic offensive that included the June 2000 summit with then-South Korean President Kim Dae Jung and a visit to Pyongyang by then-U.S. Secretary of State Madeleine Albright. Though the 2000 U.S. presidential election ended this Washington-Pyongyang rapprochement, Pyongyang nonetheless stuck by its self-imposed missile moratorium.

Strategic Restraint

For North Korea, the decision to refrain from missile tests is a strategic one. Pyongyang has carried out few tests of its ballistic missile systems (just one test each for the Nodong and Taepodong systems), though it carries out tests of short-range anti-ship and battlefield missiles fairly regularly. For Pyongyang, physical tests of weapons systems are not part of the development process but the culmination of the process itself. The country is notorious for deploying weapons systems onto the battlefield before carrying out tests on capability.

Tests are seen as more dangerous than beneficial. Pyongyang can collect information on similar missile systems from tests in Pakistan, Iran and elsewhere, but conducting the tests itself reveals its true technological capabilities — or lack thereof. Thus, a failed test could reveal a complete failure of an entire battlefield-deployed weapons system. On the other hand, ambiguity about its weapons systems — and particularly its missiles — allows Pyongyang to maintain the perception of a threat.

Under better-safe-than-sorry logic, this has left potential opponents needing to think the worst of North Korea's missiles. Thus, the range and payload of Pyongyang's rockets are almost always overestimated. Even so, without real tests, there is room to believe North Korea is not an imminent threat. This allows Pyongyang to manipulate the varying interests of surrounding nations, playing Japan off China or South Korea off the United States.

This is the same strategy North Korea uses with its nuclear program. With the end of the Cold War, North Korea lost its significance and sources of support and protection. In the early 1990s, the Pyongyang regime felt truly threatened, and thus launched its clandestine nuclear program, not revealing it until after it had already developed nuclear devices. This first nuclear crisis was a bargaining tactic, one in which Pyongyang sought to ensure regime preservation by reducing external pressures.

The 1994 Agreed Framework between Washington and Pyongyang marked the culmination of these initial efforts. Had Kim Il Sung not died at that time, North Korea's path could have been very different, as he was planning an inter-Korean summit and seeking North Korea's emergence onto the world scene. Instability and uncertainty in the transition from Kim Il Sung to Kim Jong Il short-circuited, or at least delayed, further political developments until the 2000 inter-Korean summit. This was again reversed as 9/11 changed the dynamic in Washington, making North Korea's previous negotiating tactics much less effective.

The Benefits of Ambiguity

As with its missile program, North Korea has refrained from revealing the true extent and capabilities of its nuclear program. There have been no nuclear tests, and there are unlikely ever to be such tests — unless Pyongyang has a massive arsenal of deployable weapons. For North Korea, which uses its nuclear program as a guarantor of regime survival, a nuclear test removes all ambiguity and would likely invite a pre-emptive strike while the nuclear arsenal remains small.

In fact, for North Korea, having two or three deployable and verified weapons could represent the worst position to be in. It would demonstrate the country is a clear and present danger to its neighbors (Japan and South Korea, neither of which is nuclear-armed) but it would not create a sufficient counterstrike capability. Add in the longer-range missiles, and North Korea could almost guarantee U.S. action against it.

For Pyongyang, then, retaining a sense of strategic ambiguity represents the best course. Pyongyang has threatened through second-hand sources several times to test its nuclear weapons and carry out a missile launch that would have the missile splashing down in the waters off New York City. As long as these are rhetorical threats, they are unverifiable, potential exaggerations, and North Korea's lack of follow-through creates the impression it is still willing to negotiate.

A nuclear test, or even another missile test at the wrong time, could shift the impression of a dangerous but manageable threat to one of a clear and present danger — one requiring immediate action. A failed nuclear or missile test could reveal inherent weaknesses in the North Korean system and bring about an intensified effort to undermine and remove the regime. Leaving people guessing, however, maintains enough doubt about North Korea's abilities to avoid drawing an immediate pre-emptive attack.

Safe and Sane

The regime in Pyongyang is neither crazy nor significantly faction-alized. It has demonstrated an ability to manipulate the world's major powers, and has proved immune to multiple attempts to capitalize on perceived internal rifts or leadership struggles — suggesting a degree of rationality in the regime based on the desire to preserve the elite and their families. Acting dangerous and accepting the consequent international isolation does not seriously undermine the power or privileges of North Korea's elite, since China, Russia and even South Korea have kept aid, investment and technology flowing.

Taking the next step and demonstrating that North Korea is a clear and present danger, one with a verifiable nuclear capability and a verifiable capability to deliver weapons to the United States, would invite a much more immediate response. Washington considered striking North Korea after the 1998 missile test, and that missile was not capable of reaching outlying U.S. islands. A new test coupled with a nuclear test would nearly guarantee a U.S. pre-emptive military strike, if Japan did not strike first. Ultimately, Pyongyang would not have enough of a defense capability to ensure regime survival if it triggered a new war with the United States. Even North Korean ally China has plans to effectively turn North Korea into a protectorate if another war breaks out at Pyongyang's instigation. China has even signaled this to the United States, noting that Chinese intervention in a new Korean war would be very different than it was half a century ago.

In Pyongyang, regime survival drives the decision-making process. Decisions about economic talks with South Korea, nuclear talks with the United States or new missile launches will always be carried out with this goal in mind. Though the methods of regime preservation might not make complete sense abroad, they are clearly rational from the North Korean perspective, and thus predictable.

For Pyongyang, then, any new test will be carefully examined before being carried out. Any new launch will be of a satellite-launch vehicle configuration, as with the Taepodong-1 launch, to provide just enough questions of intent and capability to avoid tipping the strategic calculus. A failed satellite launch would prove more devastating to North Korea's carefully cultivated image than no launch at all. Unless the risks change, or the regime feels an attack is imminent, the current calculus in Pyongyang still weighs against a new Taepodong launch.

Prolonging the Uncertainty
June 24, 2006

North Korea's Taepodong-2 remains sitting on the launch pad after more than a week. For much of that time, the launch site at Musudan-ri has been cloud-covered, but a break in the clouds June 22 offered a clear view of the site (seen here in this DigitalGlobe satellite image), showing little apparent activity.

It remains unclear whether North Korea actually intends to launch the Taepodong-2, or whether it has even actually fueled the missile. While the different assessments heard from a variety of sources in South Korea, the United States, Russia, China and Japan are in part colored by political considerations — Seoul is debating whether it is a missile or satellite launch, and Japan is always the first to leak that a missile is about to launch —there are technical issues as well.

First and foremost is getting accurate images. Satellites that shoot optical imagery are limited by weather and flight pattern. They are not permanently stationed over North Korea and therefore gather snapshots periodically rather than provide a constant stream of information. This leads to confusion over details such as whether or not North Korea has fueled its missile. Aircraft supplements satellites, but these are limited by distance and available time over target.

The U.S. National Reconnaissance Office has the capability to collect other information, such as signals and electronic intelligence, over the site by using different kinds of satellites. Some satellites can

NORTH KOREA'S TAEPODONG
LAUNCH SITE, JUNE 26, 2006

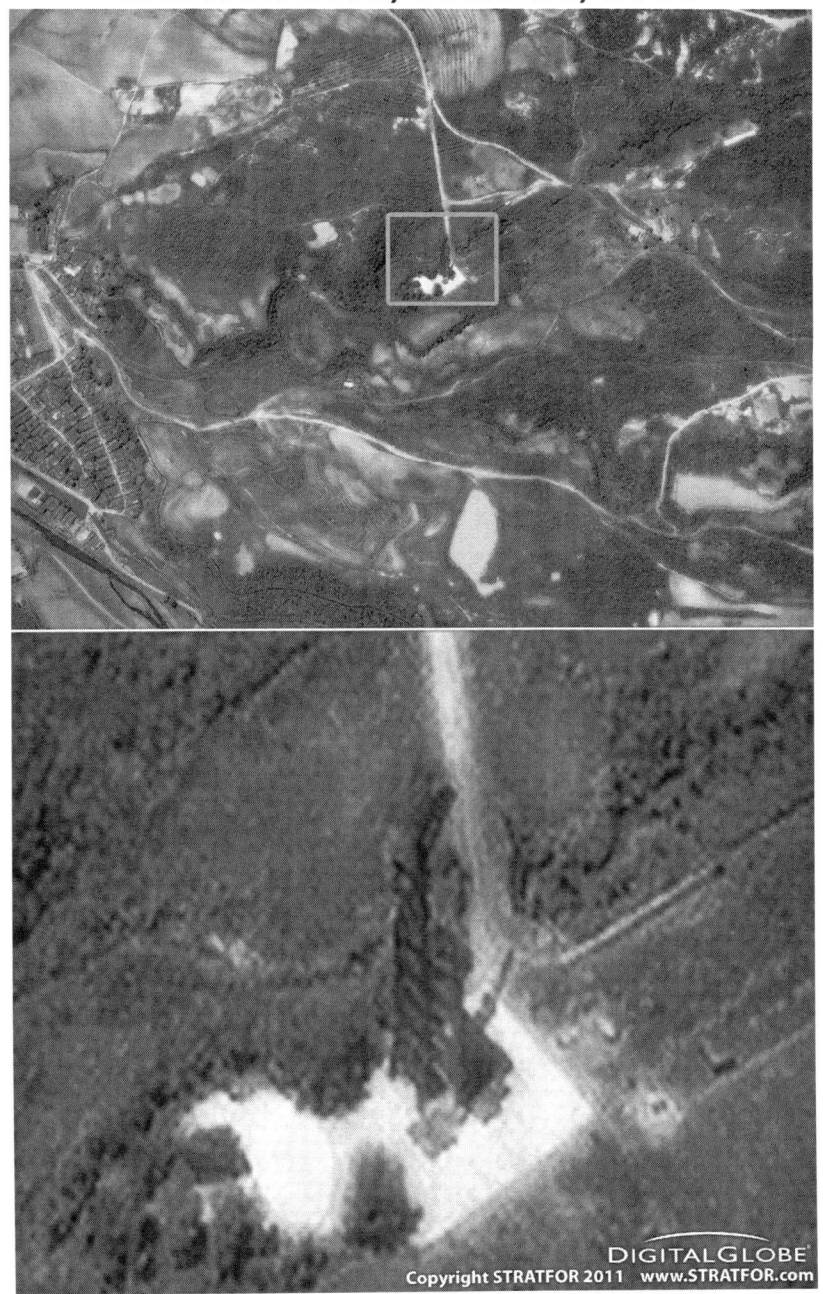

DIGITALGLOBE
Copyright STRATFOR 2011   www.STRATFOR.com

see through cloud cover using radar imagery. Using infrared imagery could indicate if the missile is fueled, as a missile with fuel in it would be much colder than its surroundings, especially in summer. Even with satellite and aerial imagery, however, it is relatively easy for the observed nation to trick the cameras. Pictures do lie, and manipulation is part of the game. North Korea is well known for playing to the satellites, presenting provocative images that may turn out to be hoaxes. Like the Quaker cannon — logs painted to look like cannons — or the Serbian plywood aircraft decoys that fooled U.S. reconnaissance efforts and U.S. pilots alike during Operation Allied Force in 1999, there are many ways to trick the observers into seeing what someone wants them to see. And if there is a desire to hide something, there are numerous methods of concealment. Part of playing to the satellites might include figuring out when they are overhead and making sure to show or not show certain things during those times.

In the North Korean case, there is also a significant lack of ground-based intelligence assets. Knowledge of the intentions or even the actual actions of the North Korean regime is more often impressionistic rather than based on information from the field. The information that does trickle out of North Korea is often colored by an agenda. For example, many groups use selective reports from North Korean dissidents and refugees for political and humanitarian purposes; whether their stories are true or not, there is little assessment of the overall situation.

The availability of information becomes a critical aspect of the final assessment. The core of the information — at least aerial and satellite surveillance — comes from the United States, and not all of it is shared with the regional allies Japan and South Korea. Tokyo has begun launching its own spy satellite program, and South Korea plans to follow suit, as both find themselves somewhat at the mercy of the United States. Seoul and Tokyo must wait for Washington to release information to them, and even if it is only a few hours' delay, it still delays the ability to formulate an assessment and prepare next steps.

This has increased Tokyo's efforts to integrate itself into the U.S. anti-missile systems and gain access to U.S. technology and real-time information. It has fueled Seoul's drive for a more independent military and intelligence capability. In both cases, there has been a coloring of the information as it is released to the public. Japan suggests a failed North Korean test that rains parts down on Japanese territory would be considered an act of war; South Korea emphasizes economic exchanges and the idea that, rather than a missile test, it is a satellite launch, something peaceful nations are all allowed to do.

And this divergence fits with North Korea's strategic calculation. The South Korean government is desperate to prove its North Korean policy has been accurate and is most concerned about the consequences of triggering a conflict with North Korea. Japan is interested in playing up the threats as Tokyo works toward a revision of its Self Defense Force, both in capabilities and in doctrine. The longer the crisis exists, the more divergent the allies may move. And this will allow Pyongyang the ability to play off of the splits.

Changing Views of Nuclear Proliferation
Dec. 19, 2006

The six-party talks on North Korea's nuclear program have restarted in Beijing, with Pyongyang demanding acceptance as the world's latest nuclear power. This is clearly a nonstarter, given the number of times the U.S. chief negotiator to the talks, Assistant Secretary of State Christopher Hill, has made clear that the United States will not accept North Korea as a nuclear power.

Perhaps coincidentally, on the same day the six-party talks resumed, U.S. President George W. Bush signed the Henry J. Hyde United States-India Peaceful Atomic Energy Cooperation Act, the formalization of the March 2 handshake agreement between Bush and Indian Prime Minister Manmohan Singh. With this deal, India gains access to nuclear technology from members of the Nuclear Suppliers Group despite its failure to accede to the Nuclear Nonproliferation Treaty. The special dispensation for New Delhi effectively ends U.S. punishment of India following its 1998 nuclear tests, when India unilaterally declared itself a nuclear weapons state.

While there are innumerable differences between India and North Korea, including their relations with the United States and their international positions, the dichotomy in U.S. action raises a question: Is it a viable assumption that nuclear states will refrain from the proliferation of nuclear weapons technology or act to prevent the spread of such systems? This becomes an even more critical question amid Iran's very public efforts to pursue civilian nuclear technology (and only thinly veiled efforts to seek nuclear weapons), and as Japan more openly confronts its own prohibition on the development of a nuclear weapons capability.

The 1945 use of nuclear weapons by the United States against Hiroshima and Nagasaki began a new era in warfare — one in which an entire enemy city could be destroyed by a single strike. This triggered a nuclear race among other major nations, with Russia testing its first nuclear weapon in 1949, followed by the United Kingdom in 1952, France in 1960 and China in 1964. Israel is believed to have gone nuclear only a few years later. In these early years of nuclear weapons development, the investment necessary to join the nuclear club — measured not only in financial terms but also in resources and brain power — was rather substantial, thus limiting the number of countries able to develop nuclear weapons.

By the 1960s, as the Cold War settled into a routine and nuclear weapons delivery systems shifted from land- and air-based to sea-based as well, completing the nuclear triad, the concept of mutually assured destruction (MAD) became well-established, in theory if not in name. The balance of nuclear power between the United States and the Soviet Union led to the building of frameworks to avoid any "accidental discharges" of nuclear weapons and to control the proliferation of such weapons (particularly following the Cuban missile crisis). As technology and resources became more readily available, more attention was paid to preventing additional countries from joining the nuclear club.

There was another spurt of nuclear activity in the 1970s by second-tier nations, including South Korea, South Africa and Iraq, as well as India and Pakistan. Seoul's program was stopped by U.S. threats to vacate the peninsula (and leave South Korea undefended against potential North Korean aggression). Baghdad's development program was cut short by an Israeli airstrike in 1981. South Africa ultimately developed and produced a few nuclear weapons (only to later disable them after the end of the apartheid era). India's nuclear program came to fruition in the 1970s, with Pakistan developing the capability to produce a weapon in the late 1980s.

With the end of the Cold War and the collapse of the Soviet Union came a new international urgency to rein in the number of nuclear weapons on the planet and constrain the number of countries that possess such systems. The only former Soviet state "allowed" to keep nuclear weapons was Russia, which, incidentally, also retained MAD parity with the United States. As if to test this new push to reduce nuclear weapons access, North Korea accelerated its program in the late 1980s, creating at least a rudimentary device by the early 1990s. This sparked the first of a series of nuclear "crises" that served as bargaining chips for the regime on the international scene — particularly in Pyongyang's relations with Washington.

As the first of these nuclear crises heated up, the United States, under then-President Bill Clinton, began preparing for a strike against North Korea — potentially with nuclear weapons. Such was the intensity with which the United States opposed the proliferation of nuclear weapons and technology. While a negotiated settlement was eventually achieved (the so-called Agreed Framework), Washington made it very clear that it would never accept North Korea as a nuclear state and threatened, even if unofficially, a first-strike option to keep Pyongyang from crossing the nuclear Rubicon by testing a device.

This threat stood for more than a decade, and it served in part to constrain North Korea's actions. For Pyongyang, ambiguity in its nuclear capability meant it had room to negotiate. Confirmation of nuclear capability was a bridge too far — something that would invite U.S. military action. North Korea wanted to be threatening enough to force negotiations, but not cross the line into being threatening enough to force military action. That line was always the testing of a weapon. In October 2006, however, that line was crossed — and the result was a resounding nothingness, aside from sanctions on iPods and expensive liquor. Something apparently had changed.

North Korea looked to the examples of India and Pakistan when making its decision to test. When India and Pakistan carried out their nuclear tests in 1998, there was an international outcry as the two states broke into the nuclear club — and a high level of concern that the already contentious relations between India and Pakistan could quickly degrade into a nuclear exchange. While the latter fear has not (yet) come true — even as India and Pakistan engaged in the 1999 Kargil conflict — what perhaps has been even more notable is the general acceptance of both India and Pakistan as nuclear states. Despite initial sanctions, strictures and demands for accession to international nuclear conventions, neither New Delhi nor Islamabad have been severely isolated or punished for breaking the taboo and testing weapons.

In part, this was because it was a known secret that India and Pakistan had developed nuclear devices and weapons even before the 1998 tests, which were more verifications than true breakthroughs in capability. But there were larger issues at play. A decade after the Cold War structures began crumbling, the United States had begun looking at India in a different light, no longer viewing it as a non-aligned nation leaning left but as a potential ally in the international arena, particularly amid growing concern over the rise of China. The United States decoupled its relations with Islamabad and New Delhi, making it clear during the Kargil crisis that there was no longer a zero-sum set of relationships.

The 9/11 attacks against the United States quickly altered Washington's slow movement away from Pakistan as well, making Islamabad's cooperation key to U.S. military operations in Afghanistan.

One of the first steps in this was to ensure that Pakistan's nuclear arsenal was secure. And this the United States did, though in a relatively low-key manner. With a handle on Pakistan's nuclear program and a need for Islamabad's continued acquiescence to U.S. operations in Afghanistan, Washington was then more free to move forward with redefining its relations with India — and accepting India's role as a nuclear-capable state. The verbal nuclear agreement between Bush and Singh in March 2006 demonstrated that a new line of thinking on U.S. nuclear policy had already taken hold.

Two key elements of U.S. nuclear policy became apparent under the post-9/11 Bush administration. First, Washington was shifting from the MAD concept to the very real possibility of using tactical nuclear weapons as practical military tools (e.g., for bunker-busting) and not just as symbols of deterrence or as weapons to destroy whole cities. The second was that Washington, while strongly opposed to proliferation, would use negotiations as a tactic to deal with existing nuclear states, and would seriously consider military operations for dealing with states attempting to develop nuclear weapons. The combination of minimal punishment for Pakistan, preferential treatment for India and the sense that proven nuclear capability would prevent pre-emptive U.S. strikes caused Pyongyang to significantly rethink its own nuclear negotiating strategy.

But Pyongyang was not alone in its decision-making process. Beijing also played a critical role, and Moscow a secondary one. Patrons from the Cold-War era, China and Russia are longtime allies of North Korea. Both states still wield a fair amount of influence on the country, and while they might not be fully able to shape North Korean behavior, they can dissuade Pyongyang from taking certain actions — such as testing a nuclear device. North Korea's July missile tests, in the face of international warnings and U.S. threats to test anti-missile systems on any North Korean launch, were a probe by both North Korea and China to see the full extent of U.S. capability and willingness to follow through on its threats. The answer was that Washington, while willing to threaten, was apparently not willing to act.

The sanctions and strongly worded statements toward North Korea after the missile tests did little but embolden Pyongyang. And Beijing supported the course of action leading toward the nuclear test — despite public protestations to the contrary. North Korea's entry into the nuclear club (whether officially accepted or not) has clearly become a de facto reality. China did not oppose the test in any meaningful way, and more likely gave tacit support. Surely Beijing could have put more pressure on North Korea if it had truly opposed the impending test. And the United States, by not reacting in any concrete way, has basically accepted the reality of a North Korean nuclear capability, six-party talks notwithstanding.

There has been a significant shift, then, in global nuclear posturing. North Korea has become a demonstrated nuclear state. While it might not have had the most successful of nuclear tests, there is little doubt that North Korea can explode a nuclear device — even if delivery options remain limited. The impact of the test on North Korea has been a few condemnations, minimally enforced sanctions and the restart of a multistate dialogue on North Korean nuclear capabilities, which gives North Korea a place at the big boys' table. There is little that could encourage or force Pyongyang to give up the nuclear capability now that it has demonstrated it.

If India can be given access to nuclear technologies despite refusing to accede to international nuclear treaties, and if North Korea can carry out a nuclear test without any punitive response, what now prevents other states, such as Iran, from accelerating their nuclear programs? And has Washington in its deal with India, and Beijing and Moscow in their tacit approval of the North Korean nuclear test, shown that public opposition to the spread of nuclear weapons is more noise than substance?

This shift in the actions of the major nuclear powers has not gone unnoticed elsewhere. Germany has effectively said it expects that the world will soon have to live with a nuclear-armed Iran, and that sanctions, while necessary, will do little to stop Iran from acquiring a nuclear capability. And Israeli Prime Minister Ehud Olmert, in his "slip" on the existence of Israeli nuclear weapons, reminded the United

States, Russia and China that Israel is not willing to accept a change in Iran's nuclear status, even if these three powers are resigned to (or are tacitly encouraging) a nuclear-armed Iran. Olmert was voicing the concern in Israel — and elsewhere — that the prohibition on the proliferation of nuclear weapons might be weakening, and that the law of nuclear deterrence may not hold if pre-emptive measures need to be taken.

This concern was also seen in outgoing U.N. Secretary-General Kofi Annan's Dec. 18 parting comments to Japan on the 50th anniversary of Tokyo's entrance into the United Nations. Annan urged Japan to stick to its non-nuclear stance, saying a country does not need nuclear weapons to achieve greatness. That Japan, the only nation to be on the receiving end of nuclear weapons, has allowed a public debate on developing nuclear weapons is perhaps the most striking example of the changing view of nuclear weapons acquisition. Tokyo wants its own nukes, even if it continues to profess a non-nuclear stance. And Japan has the capability and resources to produce nuclear weapons in short order, and the capability to deliver such weapons in a time of conflict.

And this brings us back to that post-Cold War shift in international relations. While the initial response was a rush to prevent the further proliferation of nuclear weapons to new and "rogue" states, there was another shift taking place at the same time — the tattering of the nuclear umbrella. Without the threat of global war from any regional conflict, the nuclear protection extended by the United States or the Soviets to their allies — and to states within their respective spheres of influence — was no longer a given. The major powers came to view such protection as more of a strategic cost-benefit analysis. Would Washington risk a nuclear exchange over the future of South Korea, for example, if it didn't necessarily impact the global balance with another superpower?

This concern already has been seen clearly in the realm of conventional weapons, with countries like South Korea and Japan pursuing significant arms purchases, technological advancements and military restructuring to take into account the change in the U.S.

strategic outlook. It is no surprise, then, that this concern moves into the nuclear realm as well. North Korea certainly considered its loss of ensured military support from China and Russia in its decision to pursue a nuclear program. Japan, South Korea and others are undoubtedly considering similar paths, if only in hushed voices in dimly lit rooms. And former Soviet states, particularly those in Central Asia, could be looking at their own future security and balancing their own interests between three nuclear powers — Russia, China and the United States.

Nuclear proliferation has long been an international concern — at least publicly. The transfer of technology and nuclear materials, international safeguards and inspection protocols, social and moral concerns and retaliatory fears have all played a role in keeping the number of nuclear states at a minimum. But the fear of retaliation is beginning to fade at the same time North Korea shows that even the most isolated and technologically limited of states can develop such weapons systems. And once a nation crosses the nuclear threshold, giving up nuclear weapons must be an internal choice (as seen previously in South Africa). Forcing a country to give up such weapons is only possible if one is willing to risk a nuclear exchange.

Understanding the North Korean Negotiating Style
Feb. 8, 2007

Representatives from the United States and North Korea, along with Russia, China, Japan and South Korea, will meet Feb. 8 in Beijing for the next round of talks over North Korea's nuclear program. This is the second session of the so-called six-party talks since North Korea's October 2006 nuclear test. As the participants gear up for these meetings, a sense of cautious optimism prevails — leading to a more upbeat mood than seen at most of the previous sessions.

Though the nuclear negotiations' outcome is never clear in advance, the key items on the table at this round already have been circulating through the diplomatic community, unofficial channels and the press. The basic agreement to be discussed in Beijing is the suspension of activity at North Korea's Yongbyon nuclear reactor in return for heavy fuel oil aid from the United States and other members of the six-party process. Though many more details will emerge, these two concrete steps will form the core of the negotiating session.

In looking at these negotiations, a few things should be kept in mind. First, North Korea, not the United States, initiates nuclear crises. Pyongyang uses these crises to ensure regime survival and to gain leverage with the United States, China and its other neighbors. This tactic has been used repeatedly since the early 1990s, when North Korea's erstwhile sponsors, Russia and China, turned their attention to economic relations with the West (and South Korea), rather than maintaining their socialist little brother. For Pyongyang, then, there might not be any real motivation to bring a conclusive end to the series of crises — unless North Korea's sense of national security substantially changes.

The short-term goal of the negotiations is to keep North Korea's neighbors and the United States off balance and divided while putting North Korea at the center of attention. This lets Pyongyang manipulate the differences in the national interests and political persuasions of the various players, and thus reduce the risk of military action while increasing the chances of economic and energy assistance. Though it seems counterintuitive, the plan has proved quite functional for more than a decade. Despite expectations, the North Korean regime has not collapsed — in fact, it remains firmly entrenched. And it intends to stay that way.

North Korea has delayed the resumption of six-party talks since the 2005 decision by the U.S. Treasury Department to impose Section 311 of the Patriot Act on Banco Delta Asia (BDA), a Macau-based bank accused of complicity with North Korean laundering of counterfeit money. Though the actual amount locked down by the action was small (around $24 million), the real impact came when the Treasury Department's Financial Crimes Enforcement Network blocked U.S. banks from doing business with BDA. This triggered the domino effect of foreign banks throughout Asia cutting off their North Korean accounts for fear of similar U.S. action. Both legitimate and illegitimate North Korean bank accounts were suddenly closed, and service to North Korean businesses and those doing business with North Korea was curtailed.

Pyongyang finally agreed to resume six-party nuclear talks in December 2006 after initial negotiations with the U.S. Treasury Department. Even then, the December talks dealt only with the BDA issue. Since December, there have been further meetings between North Korea and U.S. Deputy Assistant Treasury Secretary Daniel Glaser, with rumors suggesting that half of the impounded $24 million could be released and other banking avenues might be opened for North Korea. With this out of the way, Pyongyang now is preparing to make a show of progress on the nuclear front, offering to shut down Yongbyon (but not dismantle it), reactivate the cameras put in place by the International Atomic Energy Agency (IAEA) and invite IAEA inspectors back. In return, Pyongyang expects the banking sanctions issue to be resolved and for the United States to resume shipments of heavy fuel oil to North Korea.

The apparent change in the North Korean position does not mean Pyongyang is backing down or preparing to abandon its nuclear program — far from it. The nuclear program has always served as a path toward negotiations — a bargaining chip North Korea has little intention of ever truly abandoning, particularly after the October nuclear test. Instead, restarting the negotiation process now offers North Korea additional leverage, and could influence policy decisions in other concerned states.

Negotiations add strength to U.S. and South Korean arguments that communication and cooperation are better than demands and force in dealing with North Korea. This keeps North Korea in the game and allows it to keep stringing Washington, Seoul and Tokyo along with the hope that maybe the next round of talks will produce positive results. This also affects the South Korean political field, where posturing for the country's December presidential elections is in full swing. Pyongyang wants to increase the attractiveness of the south's more progressive political parties while painting the opposition Grand National Party as likely to significantly undermine the path to stability in East Asia.

A final settlement is not in the works. Instead, Pyongyang is planning a new round of progress. Washington seems aware of this, and the chief U.S. negotiator has suggested that concrete progress must be achieved in each round of talks for the meetings to continue, and that an overall settlement must be in place by early 2008 — less than a year ahead of the next U.S. presidential elections. Nonetheless, even the U.S. side has suggested that this round holds a higher chance for progress.

One factor that has contributed to the slightly elevated (though still reserved) expectations for this round of talks is the expansion of pre-talks between the United States and North Korea, as well as several other bilateral discussions among the various parties. All negotiations with North Korea face an inherent problem before the parties even sit down at the table: North Korean negotiators are not negotiators at all; they simply come with a prearranged set of demands and a very narrow set of acceptable outcomes. Put simply, they have little room to maneuver, and do not have the authority to make the necessary compromises needed in difficult negotiations.

The North Korean decision-making process is still extremely top-heavy. All critical decisions must be made at the level of Kim Jong Il. While diplomats and representatives of the state are sent abroad for discussions, their room to compromise is extremely constrained. They simply go out to put forward the latest proposals from Pyongyang, hear counterproposals and send all of this information back to the capital.

This has happened during previous multilateral forums, with North Korean negotiators cabling back to Pyongyang each afternoon or evening and coming in the next day with a new set of requirements, limits and expectations. But for this round of talks, U.S. and North Korean negotiators have been holding several rounds of bilateral pre-meetings. There has been extensive diplomatic contact between Washington and Pyongyang, Washington and Beijing, Pyongyang and Beijing, Pyongyang and Moscow and — to a lesser extent — between these players and representatives from South Korea and Japan. In addition, each side has released trial balloons and leaked its limits and openings to various proposals through semiofficial and unofficial channels.

Coming into this round, then, there has been plenty of time for each party to prepare for the others' offers and counteroffers, and for North Korea and the United States to refine their respective positions — with authority from Pyongyang. Though this does not guarantee results, it does substantially improve the prospects for progress. In the end, though, North Korean decisions are made at the top. Like the 1994 talks between Jimmy Carter and former North Korean President Kim Il Sung, the potential for major shifts in policy and direction resides only with the supreme leadership.

The Important Leap from Crisis Management
Feb. 14, 2007

The latest session of the six-party talks on North Korea's nuclear ambitions wrapped up Feb. 13 with a new agreement laying out next steps for the dismantlement of Pyongyang's nuclear program. The agreement, in short, sets a 60-day timeline for North Korea to shut down the Yongbyon nuclear plant (including the reprocessing facilities) and for the United States, China, Russia and South Korea to supply the equivalent of 50,000 tons of heavy fuel oil (which could include food or other types of aid as well). Japan has bowed out of supporting the initial tranche of aid for domestic reasons.

Unlike the Sept. 19, 2005, Joint Statement, the new agreement sets out some concrete steps toward the ultimate goal of the dismantlement of North Korea's nuclear capability, including the listing by

North Korea of its nuclear sites and the establishment of separate working groups to discuss energy aid and the normalization of relations among North Korea, Japan and the United States.

Specifics aside, this new deal changes the tenor of negotiations with North Korea from this point forward. It institutionalizes the process and removes some of the individual "spoilers" from the broader group negotiations, thus taking what has been a crisis management issue and changing it into a diplomatic engagement on security, political and economic issues.

The Feb. 13 agreement begins by referring to, but not repeating, the goal of the Sept. 15 Joint Statement, which says, "The six parties unanimously reaffirmed that the goal of the six-party talks is the verifiable denuclearization of the Korean Peninsula in a peaceful manner." The new agreement is based on this and a reference to the promise to supply energy to North Korea as stated in the Sept. 15 statement. But this agreement goes several steps beyond the September statement, requiring all parties to take actions within 60 days in order to demonstrate a commitment to the process.

Rather than one side making a gesture and the other following, each of these steps is set to begin (or, in some cases, be completed) within 60 days:

- North Korea shuts down the Yongbyon facility, including the reprocessing unit, and invites International Atomic Energy Agency inspectors back to the site.

- North Korea begins discussing the list of all of its nuclear programs.

- North Korea and the United States restart the process of normalizing relations. Washington takes steps to remove sanctions imposed under the Trading with the Enemy Act and begins removing North Korea from the State Sponsors of Terrorism list.

- North Korea and Japan resume talks aimed at normalizing relations.

- The five parties aside from North Korea agree to supply energy and economic aid to North Korea, with an emergency shipment of the equivalent of 50,000 tons of heavy fuel oil to take place within the 60-day window.

This 60-day window requires actions of each party while not requiring any party to be seen as making a bilateral concession to another. This might be semantics, but it eliminates the tit-for-tat battle over who has to blink first. To ensure that the process moves forward, the six parties have agreed to meet again in 30 days.

Perhaps more important than this initial commitment phase is the establishment of five working groups that will address certain side issues. These are part of the six-party process, but operate separately from the broader talks, keeping some of the bilateral spoilers of the multilateral forum off to the side while allowing smaller focused groups the ability to work out contentious details before bringing them to the higher-level six-party talks.

The five working groups are: a bilateral U.S.-North Korean group on the normalization of relations, a bilateral Japanese-North Korean group on the normalization of relations, a Russian-led group on the development of a "Northeast Asia Peace and Security Mechanism," a South Korean-led group on economy and energy cooperation, and a group (likely led by China) on the denuclearization of the Korean Peninsula.

By hiving these off, issues like Japan's ongoing spat with North Korea over the kidnapping of Japanese citizens in the past can be dealt with separately and thus not undermine the broader progress or movement on other issues. It also makes each of the five parties (aside from North Korea) responsible for a section of the broader picture. China retains control over the overall process (and ultimately, if there is going to be future progress, China will be critical for verification). Russia gains a role in East Asia as a moderator among China, Japan and the United States, while South Korea gains additional influence over the development of economic and energy infrastructure in North Korea — a critical step in the path toward eventual unification.

In some sense, this weakens the North Korean bargaining position, since in the past it could sink all progress by blaming it on a single party. But Pyongyang gains the institutionalization of the six-party process. The new framework takes this out of the "crisis management" basket and places it on the level of routine diplomatic management. North Korea gains the permanent attention and ear of the various players, remains the central issue in the region and thus achieves its goal in its nuclear program — economic and energy support and regime survival.

This marks a substantive shift in the overall nuclear negotiations with North Korea. Though the ultimate goal remains the "verifiable denuclearization of the Korean Peninsula," there is now an acceptance of the North Korean regime as a viable negotiating partner, as something to engage rather than something to punish and contain. That brings North Korea to the table not just as a threat to be dealt with but as a dialogue partner — a major shift in how the United States views the North Korean situation.

In some sense, this repeats the pattern of U.S.-North Korean relations under the government of former U.S. President Bill Clinton, which started out extremely acrimonious and ended with direct diplomatic engagement. The groundwork is being laid for a similar path with North Korea, though this time without any required timelines (like the 1994 Agreed Framework) to constrain the dialogue with an all-or-nothing requirement. Instead, this is an open-ended agreement. If progress is not made, North Korea gets no further assistance (at least assuming all parties follow the agreement). If Pyongyang cooperates, it gets more energy and economic aid and political recognition.

In institutionalizing the dialogue, the North Korean nuclear issue now moves into the realm of the routine. That does not mean all problems are resolved. It does not address the earlier demands by the KEDO consortium that North Korea repay the debt for KEDO's construction work on the never-completed light-water nuclear reactors as part of the 1994 Agreed Framework. Nor does it make explicit reference to North Korea's nuclear weapons (though it does mention identifying the location/status of plutonium extracted from fuel rods, so that could include the nuclear devices). And it does not set solid dates or mechanisms for verifiable denuclearization. It leaves these issues for the working groups and the broader six-party talks in the future.

Though there are many unanswered questions, there is now action by all parties to move out of crisis mode and into the diplomatic (and some would say bureaucratic) mode. For Washington, this offers some evidence of a foreign policy "victory," or at least a demonstration of foreign policy without the use of force. For North Korea, it once again shows that Pyongyang's nuclear program is and continues to be a bargaining tool, rather than an offensive tool.

For Seoul, this is a vindication of the engagement policy, and lays the groundwork for greater economic and energy development in North Korea and between the two Koreas, building up the North in preparation for future unification. For Russia, this marks a return to the broader issues of East Asian security. For Japan, it is a way to continue to hound North Korea on the abduction issue as long as domestic politics require it, all without facing pressure from the United States to back down. And for China, Beijing once again plays the central role in the denuclearization and regional proliferation issues, retaining leverage needed for dealing with the United States.

In 30 days, the parties will meet again to check progress. There is always room for one or more parties simply to refuse to comply, and many pitfalls lie ahead — but the sense of crisis is fading and the routinization setting in.

Of Rail Links and Maritime Borders
May 2, 2007

North Korea responded May 2 to a call by South Korea two days earlier to schedule general-level defense talks ahead of a planned May 17 test of the two inter-Korean rail lines. The agreement to test the rail lines came during the 13th meeting of the Inter-Korean Economic Cooperation Promotion Committee, which concluded April 22. The two Koreas have planned previous tests of the rail lines, but each was complicated by a lack of security assurances and the North ultimately cancelled them.

The inter-Korean rail lines are a critical part of South Korea's long-term plans for Korean integration and building a unified Korea as an economic and trade hub in East Asia. There are currently two inter-Korean rail lines: the Kyonggi line running along the west coast linking Seoul and Pyongyang and extending into China, and the Donghae line linking Pusan and Wonsan and extending into Russia. When fully operational, the rail system will allow land transportation between South Korea and Europe via Russia, China and Central Asia — the so-called Iron Silk Road.

While interested, North Korea has been less focused on the rail links than South Korea. Pyongyang initially was reticent to open up the demilitarized zone (DMZ), remove land mines and defensive equipment and allow the opening of what some saw as at worst an invasion corridor and at best a ready pipeline for South Korean propaganda and subversion. But this view has been overshadowed somewhat by the prospect of economic benefits flowing from the land-based linkages. Highways that parallel the two inter-Korean rail lines have been used to transit goods and workers between South Korea and the North Korean economic zone in Kaesong, and on the east the highway now serves as a link between South Korea and the North Korean tourist resort at Mount Kumgang.

But Pyongyang is still concerned about the longer and more permanent corridors the rail lines will create. For its part, North Korea is much more interested in maritime links than in land routes, as they are more defensible, more readily isolated from the bulk of North Korea's population and relatively easy to shut down for short periods of time if necessary. Pyongyang has been expanding port facilities, particularly in Nampo on its west coast, just down the Taedong River from Pyongyang. But for years, North Korea has sought to develop and open its deep-water port facilities in Haeju on its southwest coast.

INTER-KOREAN RAIL LINES

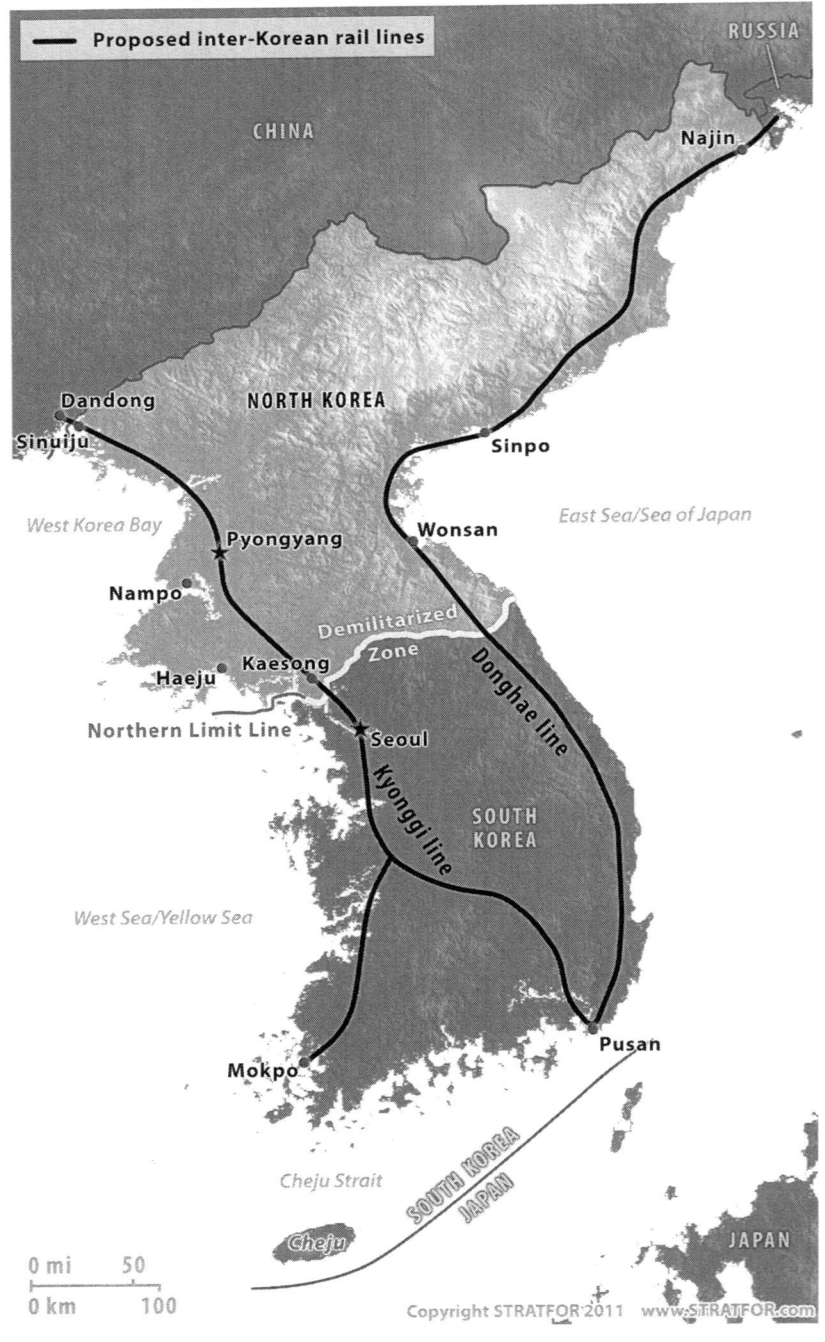

Proposed inter-Korean rail lines

RUSSIA

CHINA

NORTH KOREA

Najin

Dandong

Sinuiju

Sinpo

West Korea Bay

Pyongyang

Wonsan

East Sea/Sea of Japan

Nampo

Demilitarized

Zone

Donghae line

Haeju

Kaesong

Northern Limit Line

Seoul

Kyonggi line

SOUTH
KOREA

West Sea/Yellow Sea

Pusan

Mokpo

Cheju Strait

SOUTH KOREA
JAPAN

JAPAN

Cheju

0 mi   50

0 km   100

Copyright STRATFOR 2011   www.STRATFOR.com

Pyongyang has considered Haeju an ideal spot for a new special economic zone, but also wants to use the port facilities there in association with Kaesong-made products and as a south-facing shipping and fishing port.

The Northern Limit Line (NLL), a maritime extension of the DMZ that divides the two Koreas, poses a problem, however. Established in 1953, the NLL runs along the southern North Korean coast, giving South Korea control of a series of islands and limiting the approach for North Korean ships to Haeju, forcing them to follow a circuitous detour around the NLL. Pyongyang has brought up the possibility of redrawing the NLL several times, and while it largely abides by the imaginary line, North Korea officially refuses to accept the demarcation. Naval clashes between South Korea and North Korea in the West Sea (Yellow Sea) were in part instigated by Pyongyang to trigger new talks on the NLL. And in previous discussions of rail security, Pyongyang broached the NLL issue only to have Seoul wave the topic aside.

North Korea is now preparing to raise the NLL issue again and will use Seoul's intense interest in testing the rail lines as leverage. North Korea's recent appointment of Kim Yong Il, former minister of maritime and land transport, as prime minister reflects Pyongyang's growing interest in expanding its own maritime trade, and access to Haeju — which would require changing the NLL — increasingly will be an important issue for North Korean negotiators. Seoul is not yet prepared to change the maritime border, however, as the NLL keeps North Korean vessels far from Inchon, at the mouth of the Han River.

But there could be some concessions in the future. In August 2005, Seoul allowed North Korean ships to traverse the Cheju Strait, which lies between the southern tip of South Korea and the southern island of Cheju — a first since the Korean War. That could set a precedent for North Korean ships to gain conditional access to South Korean waters, allowing passage to Haeju without eliminating the NLL. This might not be enough of a guarantee for North Korea, but it would mark a further shift in the economic relations between the two sides.

The North Korean Development Model?
Nov. 1, 2007

North Korea is on a foreign relations charm offensive in East Asia. Prime Minister Kim Yong Il is taking the "investment and trade with North Korea" road show through Southeast Asia, and Kim Jong Il himself has suggested that North Korea might use Vietnam as a benchmark model for reviving its decrepit economy. The Chinese weekly Yazhou Zhoukan reported Oct. 28 that the North Korean leader raised the suggestion when receiving Nong Duc Manh, general secretary of Vietnam's Communist Party, in Pyongyang the week before.

North Korea is aligned with the goals of the Vietnamese growth model, but it plans to embark on its own strategy — characterized by isolated and strategically located special economic zones (SEZs). Like Vietnam, it wants economic growth without political change, except its desire to prevent the latter is even stronger. Any foreign investor wanting to play inside its borders will have to wear a political straitjacket to gain entry.

Aside from securing inflows of hard cash, economic regeneration is the most effective way for North Korea to break away from reliance on Chinese resources. Though Pyongyang might appear to be using the current "progress" in the six-party talks to establish active trade links that will take effect as soon as possible, its quest for an economic development model is not new.

Though Vietnam is being touted as the "benchmark model," it is a model of convenience. It is the real-life economy that comes closest to what Pyongyang considers an ideal model — namely, one that has minimal impact on the regime's tight social and political control but still allows for an increase in foreign investment inflows.

The North Korean regime abhorred what happened in the Soviet Union with perestroika and, despite its initial enthusiasm for Deng Xiaoping's "open up to get rich" model, it has become increasingly nervous about how the devolution of economic authority has eroded Beijing's central political command.

Vietnam's "Doi Moi" model, however, has been tweaked and amended in recent years in order to avoid any form of social or political change (or at least to stave it off for a very long time). It was initially adopted in the mid-1980s to overcome international isolation and economic crisis — with the country's survival as the primary goal — before being tweaked again in the early 1990s (concurrent with the communist bloc's collapse) to preserve party-state power and guarantee the Communist Party's survival — goals that appeal to North Korea's leader and prime minister.

Until the Cold War ended, Marxist ideals held sway in North Korea; capitalism and entrepreneurship were criminal, and private trade was persecuted with fervor. Such an ideological environment, however, depended on North Korea having a resource-rich and generous neighbor with an active interest in propping it up: China. But as Beijing turned inward to focus on economic reforms in the early 1990s, and moved to formalize ties with South Korea while pressuring Pyongyang to do the same, a rift between North Korea and its giant neighbor began to grow. North Korea initially considered following in China's economic footsteps, but caution stopped any follow-up action. As Pyongyang drifted lower on Beijing's list of priorities, so did the predictability of its supplies from China.

North Korean economic reforms first began in 1992 under the watchful gaze of former leader Kim Il Sung. These subsequently stalled as a result of his death in 1994, after which his son consolidated control and the country regressed into economic and political isolation. Economic reforms were frozen for five years. They resumed in 1999 but failed to deliver the diplomatic engagement and economic opportunities Kim Jong Il hoped for, due largely to the vast changes in the United States' geopolitical outlook after 2001. As economic desperation has intensified in recent years, Pyongyang has become increasingly active in its courtship of foreign investors, driving it into a new phase of global interaction.

North Korea's current economic model can best be explained as consisting of two stages. The ultimate goal is to attract enough foreign capital inflows and trade for North Korea to develop into a regional hub similar to many of its Asian neighbors — but one in which all trade takes place inside strictly isolated areas. Setting up various strategically located SEZs is the first step. Attracting foreign-capital inflows that Pyongyang can use as it pleases is the second.

SEZs as Launch Pads

The best-known SEZ is Kaesong. Located on the North Korean-South Korean border, this zone is heavy with political implications but offers little attraction to non-South Korean foreign investors, given its inland location. A key feature of the current inter-Korean negotiations, it is populated mostly by small- to medium-sized South Korean-subsidized firms producing low-end consumer products such as clothes, shoes and watches. Its 2006 revenue amounted to $74 million, which boosted the value of inter-Korean commercial transactions. It is mostly underwritten by the South Koreans, who have the most to gain politically from its success.

North Korea learned the importance of geographical location from its very first SEZ, which started in Rajin-Sonbong to the northeast. The isolated location on the Tumen River was accessible only to a handful of Chinese and Russian businessmen. After the SEZ disintegrated into a casino haven, Pyongyang shut it down. The second SEZ sat on the Chinese border, at the mouth of the Yalu River, in a town called Sinuiju. This was a good location, offering easy access to China's consumer markets and to dependable rail/ship transportation infrastructure. Even Beijing realized the viability of this zone as a potential competitive threat to its own export businesses and put a quick stop to it in 2006 by arresting the Chinese entrepreneur who was the driving force behind it. In spite of this hiccup, Pyongyang has since announced plans to continue with the SEZ's opening.

Other possible SEZ locations include Wonson, Nampo and Haeju — all of which are industrial port cities strategically located for quick shipment of goods to China or Japan. Pyongyang's plan is to eventually push all SEZs toward deepwater ports, where it can take fullest advantage of its proximity to some of the world's busiest trading countries.

The main deterrent for any prospective foreign investor is the political risk surrounding Washington and Pyongyang. This risk is epitomized by the recent Banco Delta Asia saga, in which a Macao-based bank was slapped with U.S. financial sanctions for handling North Korean government clients' funds. The follow-on effect this move had on the reputations of Banco Delta Asia's other (U.S. and non-U.S.) clients was a stark reminder of how U.S. financial clout can affect the profitability of any business connected directly or indirectly to a "rogue" regime. And of course, there is always the risk that Pyongyang could cease to cooperate with foreign investors. The North Korean leadership has no electorate to answer to, and the quality and reliability of its workforce remains untested.

To counter this, Pyongyang is making a heavy sell of its guaranteed pool of cheap, disciplined labor; central accessibility to road, rail and shipping transportation routes; and a location next door to some of the world's largest consuming economies.

The purpose of these SEZs is to bring in investment, technology and training without exposing North Korea's populace to Western influences, and without more than a trickle of skills and capital seeping out into the wider country. Each zone is walled off from neighboring cities, with workers cordoned off in housing within North Korean government work facilities. Pyongyang maintains maximum political and social control by being the only gateway through which any wage exchange or employee selection is conducted. North Korea will employ handpicked workers who will, in a controlled environment, become more efficient and skilled in manufacturing design and methods. Pyongyang will transfer these skills — but only via workers who are considered the most politically reliable — to workplaces elsewhere in North Korea in order to bring about "indigenous" improvements, or to facilities that train North Korean workers. Foreign investors will have little to no control over their workforces.

Foreign Investment in North Korea

Outside of the SEZs, the majority of foreign investors inside North Korea fall into one of these categories:

- Politically driven groups (South Korean government-sponsored businesses).
- High risk-taking individual investors and North Korean political/financial specialists who are seeking opportunities and awaiting a change in the political dynamic.
- Joint-venture consortium funds that spread the risk of each investment deal among multiple foreign investors.
- Oil and natural gas companies hungry to tap the potential wealth of resources (e.g., onshore/offshore oil, uranium, tungsten, gold) that have yet to be fully explored north of the peninsula.

Most of these investors are Chinese, South Korean or European. In Pyongyang, Siemens has an office, a Swiss-led consortium operates a business school (Pyongyang Business School, which reportedly started in September with 150 MBA candidates), and an Italian international law firm (Birindelli e Associati) assists foreign clients considering investing in the country.

Enthusiasm for speculative investing in North Korea began to grow in the early 2000s, and though positive rates of return cannot yet be guaranteed — nor can rates competitive with those found in Vietnam or China — speculation is steadily accumulating. Even Nestle's CEO is rumored to have made a bid for a North Korean ice cream brand.

Investment funds continue to pop up (such as the U.K.-based Chosun Fund or Global Panel's North Korea Investment Fund), coming up with innovative ways of insuring against mass expropriation (e.g., investing in individual transactions rather than direct asset ownership).

The key problems with Pyongyang's grand SEZ-driven model are the lack of trust between foreign investors and the host government and the lack of a sufficiently large, skilled and educated labor force. Only a tiny portion of the population is allowed to work — under stringent government restrictions — which means that if demand suddenly peaks, foreign investors' ability to ramp up production (with overtime or additional hires) will be severely limited.

Given North Korea's history of famine, ideological education and inefficient use of labor, the country has not shown an ability to provide competent workers with the flexibility and adaptability that modern businesses demand. Besides capital, multinationals will need to bring in foreign workers (and their social influences) to make it worth their while, probably beyond the strict limits envisioned by the Pyongyang regime.

With that in mind, there is a high probability that, despite all the talk of SEZs, North Korea will have to rely first on its resource-driven projects (i.e., mines) and not work-driven projects (i.e., SEZs) to attract foreign capital. Establishing walled-off community compounds that house workers around mining areas — as in South Africa — offers the immediate source of hard cash and relative social isolation Pyongyang wants but without the transfer of skills to its labor force.

If the current progress being made on six-party nuclear talks continues and North Korea's nuclear reactor really shuts down before year's end, it would not be incorrect to say that political risk for potential foreign investors in North Korea has fallen. But while foreign investment in North Korea is no longer an impossible idea, it is too soon to predict that North Korea will join the next wave of foreign direct investment hot spots in Asia. For now, the only sectors that can be guaranteed both foreign investor interest and entry are energy and raw materials, including oil, gold and timber. In these areas, investors of Swiss, South Korean, British and New Zealand origin already have jumped onto the exploration bandwagon.

Pyongyang's U.S. Hopes

North Korea is counting on using the SEZs to prove to foreign investors that it is a destination worth investing in, even if uncertainty continues to linger in the form of political conflict with the United States. Though a positive return on investment will not appear until the U.S.-North Korean situation stabilizes, Pyongyang is pinning its hopes on being removed from the U.S. terrorism list in order to end the associated sanctions. This could come as early as the end of the year if talks continue progressing at the current pace.

Ultimately, because of the political implications of such a move, U.S.-North Korean relations probably will not be normalized for some time. But even if North Korea plans ahead and gets its first SEZ stage off the ground, and even if a U.S. economic liaison office is set up in Pyongyang, mass foreign investment is not likely to surge. North Korea's political straitjacket will deter not only political subversion but also foreign investor entry.

The End of Crisis Diplomacy?
March 28, 2008

North Korea is once again seeking to stir up a crisis: testing several surface-to-ship missiles March 28 in the West Sea, warning that U.S. insistence on disclosure of its uranium program (rather than just its plutonium program) could stall or end progress on the dismantling of North Korea's already-declared nuclear facilities, and kicking South Korean government officials out of the Kaesong joint economic zone. But so far, no one is biting Pyongyang's crisis bait. The North Korean leadership might be learning the limits of its crisis diplomacy.

For nearly two decades (since the collapse of its Cold War patron system), North Korea has survived well beyond the expectations of many analysts. In fact, the country and its regime haven't simply survived. Through a series of carefully scripted nuclear and missile "crises" and the exploitation of differences in policy and security sensitivities among their neighbors and between their neighbors and the United States, they also have been able to remain relevant and shape and constrain the actions of "big" nations. These include the United States, China, Russia and Japan, as well as South Korea, of course.

Other Soviet allies saw their regimes change or their significance fade after the collapse of the Soviet Union. But North Korea's location — near China, Japan and Russia and across the Demilitarized Zone from tens of thousands of U.S. forces in South Korea — and the fact that Asia was one of the most dynamically changing and expanding regions at the time allowed Pyongyang to succeed where many of its contemporaries failed. North Korea defied the odds, employing what STRATFOR in 1999 dubbed the "Crazy Fearsome Cripple Gambit."

This strategy involves three interlinking pieces:

- Be crazy: North Korea projected an international image of a crazy, reclusive regime — one that just might be suicidal enough to take on the United States in a conventional or even nuclear confrontation. North Korea worked very hard to appear unpredictable.

- Be fearsome: North Korea showed off its real, imaginary or potential military might by exposing its nuclear work, conducting missile tests and military exercises, issuing extreme rhetoric and, in October 2006, through its most extreme action — a nuclear test.

- Be crippled: Despite its constant military posturing, North Korea economically is considered a failed state, a country that since the 1990s has not been able to feed its own people and always appears to be teetering on the edge of a social rebellion or a complete political collapse.

Taken together, this strategy makes North Korea too dangerous to ignore, but too weak and unpredictable to take strong action against. Instead, the world has tried over and over to manage the North Korea issue, waiting for the "inevitable" collapse of the regime. And each time things settle down, North Korea stirs up a new crisis.

But when the United States lost interest in playing Pyongyang's game after the 9/11 attacks, North Korea began a series of escalating steps to try to regain attention. These culminated in the July 2006 missile tests and October 2006 nuclear test — an action that had long been thought of as a red line that North Korea would not cross and the United States would not tolerate. The nuclear test ultimately led to the resumption of talks with North Korea, which put into motion the dismantling of the North's nuclear facilities and included promises of economic aid and the potential for diplomatic recognition.

But in testing a nuclear device, North Korea played its last and most extreme crisis card. And the world's reaction was much more blasé than its response to the North's 1998 missile launch. North Korea had begun seeing the limits of crisis diplomacy. Stirring up a crisis before negotiations allows the North to shape the talks and keep them focused primarily on returning the situation to the pre-crisis status quo in return for benefits, aid and promises to Pyongyang. But the current set of six-party nuclear talks has slipped from crisis mode to bureaucratic negotiations. North Korea is losing leverage.

Pyongyang failed to meet its December 2007 deadline to release a list of its nuclear facilities and programs. North Korea claimed it had given full disclosure, but Washington insisted on information about not only the well-known plutonium program but also the uranium program and proliferation activities. Pyongyang stalled, but rather than creating a sense of crisis, Washington portrayed the move as simply a bureaucratic hiccup. Because stalling failed to change the tone and backroom negotiations are continuing, Pyongyang has again tried to create a sense of crisis with its latest moves. But the South Koreans are not reacting. The new government in Seoul is showing its resolve not to give in to what some in the United States and abroad have labeled as North Korean "nuclear blackmail."

The fact that North Korea has resorted to its previous brinksmanship is a signal that Pyongyang is nearly ready to re-enter talks and wants to have some added leverage. There have been numerous rumors of a tacit deal between North Korea and the United States to have either a phased disclosure or two lists — a public plutonium one and a secret uranium and proliferation one. Pyongyang seems amenable to these options, but does not want to come into the talks giving Washington the initiative. Thus it seeks to stir a sense of immediacy and a fear that all the progress to date could be lost without concessions from the United States or other players in the six-party process.

But Washington, Seoul and even Beijing are growing weary of Pyongyang's repeated use of crisis diplomacy. This crisis fatigue was seen most vividly in the near lack of response to North Korea's nuclear test. Pyongyang played what it thought was its most powerful card, only to find it had laid down a joker. If a North Korean nuclear test could not cause the world to react, lobbing a few anti-ship missiles off its shore is certainly not going to get anyone's blood pumping. North Korea is reaching the limits of crisis diplomacy, and after two decades it might finally have to develop a new plan.

Initiating Another Strategic Crisis
Feb. 3, 2009

North Korea might be preparing another test of the Taepodong-series long-range ballistic missile, South Korean and Japanese media have reported, citing regional and U.S. intelligence and satellite imagery. Pyongyang is apparently preparing to launch the latest version of the Taepodong from its newest missile facility in the northwest Korean Peninsula to place a satellite in orbit in a repeat of its 1998 attempt. The latest move comes as Pyongyang has stepped up its rhetoric against Seoul, and warned Washington that the nuclear deterrent is more important to North Korea than normalized relations with the United States.

Rumors of preparation at the new North Korean missile site have been circulating in Washington, Seoul, Beijing and Tokyo since the second half of 2008. This is due less to some breakthrough in intelligence collection on North Korea than to Pyongyang intentionally not disguising its activities at the site. The latest warnings of an imminent missile test are based on satellite images of a train carrying a long, cylindrical object fairly certain to be a Taepodong missile. For North Korea, it is not the secrecy or surprise in a test launch that matters, but rather the advance warning of tests. Combined with its latest rhetorical outbursts and withdrawal from the inter-Korean agreements on security and borders, Pyongyang is signaling once again that it is a dangerous, unpredictable nation that needs to be dealt with quickly — but it is doing so in a rather predictable manner.

In many ways, North Korea's behavior is not all that surprising. Pyongyang has long used threats and escalations to garner attention and concessions from its neighbors and the United States. It carefully makes threats and warnings of escalating actions long before it actually takes the warned-of action, in hopes that fear of the action will trigger counteroffers from its neighbors and Washington to prevent it from actually taking the step. The lead-up to the 2006 North Korean nuclear test followed this warn-warn-warn-act pattern, with stairstep escalations of everything from withdrawing from the Nuclear Non-proliferation Treaty to the actual test itself, each action repeatedly telegraphed before it was carried out.

Once again, North Korea has followed this pattern. Its recent announcement on considering the inter-Korean agreements on security and border issues null is not a sudden or unexpected move, but the result of a series of prior warnings as Pyongyang slowly raised the stakes.

This time around, Pyongyang has been motivated in part by its initial problem with the administration of South Korean President Lee Myung Bak, a problem in some ways similar to its initial problems with the Bush administration when it first took office. Lee refused fully to acknowledge agreements between the previous South Korean president and North Korea, instead calling the south's entire North Korean policy into review. In particular, Pyongyang complained that Lee failed to follow through with economic agreements promised by then-outgoing South Korean President Roh Moo Hyun in an October 2007 summit, or to build on the June 2000 summit agreements between North Korean leader Kim Jong Il and then-South Korean President Kim Dae Jung.

North Korea sees the accords signed with previous South Korean or U.S. governments as much more binding than Seoul or Washington perhaps see them. While presidents, political parties and policy initiatives change regularly in democracies, in North Korea, these accords were reached only with the direct involvement of Kim, who despite his recent illness has not left power nor altered his fundamental stance in negotiations abroad. Pyongyang still struggles with the idea that locking in a policy with the outgoing president of a foreign country does not necessarily lock in the policy or agreements. To adjust for this, it reverts to its tried-and-true method of seeking to create a sense of crisis, forcing the other side back to the table and moving Pyongyang closer to its political, security and economic goals.

In the case of South Korea, Pyongyang warned that failure to accede to the Oct. 4, 2007, and June 15, 2000, declarations would leave border security responsibilities impossible for the North to fulfill, and put the Mount Kumgang tourism project and the Kaesong joint economic zone at risk. After a series of intensifying warnings, operations first at Kumgang and then at Kaesong were significantly curtailed as Pyongyang closed off the border. When that failed to get the desired response, Pyongyang began warning that other inter-Korean accords were up in the air, and that South Korea was pushing the two halves of the peninsula closer to war. This, in turn, presaged the most recent warning: the effective nullification of inter-Korean accords on security and borders, with a not-so-subtle reference to the dispute over the boundary lines in the West (Yellow) Sea, the so-called Northern Limit Line (NLL).

The NLL has long been a sore spot for North Korea, as it effectively blocks access to the country's southern deepwater port of Haeju, as well as splitting the rich crab-fishing grounds. North and South Korea have fought two deadly naval battles in the area in recent years, the first in June 1999 and the second in June 2002. Both occurred at the height of crab season (which runs from April through June), when fishing boats from both Koreas regularly violate the maritime boundary and patrol boats from both sides more actively interdict trespassing vessels. North Korea has effectively warned that barring a rapid change in South Korean behavior, it is prepared to instigate another West Sea naval battle during crab season this year.

At the same time, Pyongyang is sending a parallel signal to Washington in a bid to force the new Obama administration to see the North Korea issue as a crisis on par with Iraq, Iran and Afghanistan — though much more easily defused with cooperation and concessions. Again, Pyongyang wants to force Washington into negotiations beneficial to North Korea at little cost to the North Korean state. Creating a well-planned crisis is a way to do so, and Pyongyang's past behavior (the 2006 nuclear test) clearly demonstrates that it is not simply bluffing. Preparation for a missile launch, highly noticeable on the spy satellites that continuously monitor North Korea, is both a warning and an offer to Washington.

From the North Korean perspective, a missile test, most likely in the form again of an attempted satellite launch, could create a new set of crises for Washington. Not only would it continue to stir debate over North Korea policy on the domestic front, it also could tear at the relations between Washington and its regional allies, which will question why the United States did not intervene to prevent the launch. More significantly, it could cause problems beyond the region. The Obama administration is rethinking U.S. ballistic missile defense (BMD) plans in Europe, but a North Korean launch will reinvigorate proponents of the plan. BMD plans have major implications for U.S. relations with Russia and China (especially with regard to Japanese participation in the latter case).

Not coincidentally, North Korea is setting up the very real potential of both a missile test and a clash in the West Sea at around the same time, between April and June, in order to create a real sense of regional crisis. As before, North Korea is clearly signaling its course of action several times, offering a "way out" for the target of its bellicosity. But it also generally follows through when it wants to make a point. And the very threats and warnings of unpredictability and danger that North Korea uses to gain concessions also keep the United States and others from pursuing military solutions to the North Korean problem, for fear of a much larger war.

North Korea is seeking to set itself high on the agenda of the new U.S. administration, testing the resolve of the incoming president to find the red line. (However, as Pyongyang has seen with its nuclear test, this red line can be a moving target.) North Korea is raising a crisis at a time when its primary targets — Washington, Seoul and Tokyo — are all struggling with the economic crisis. Moreover, the United States is struggling with Iraq and Afghanistan, while the leaders of South Korea and Japan are suffering from flagging popularity ratings. North Korea's current brinksmanship offers it an easy way out of a new crisis: concessions for a return to the status quo.

The Politics of Kaesong
May 15, 2009

North Korea's Central Special Development Guidance Bureau declared "the nullification of all incumbent regulations and contracts regarding the Kaesong industrial complex" May 15, in an announcement broadcast by the official (North) Korean Central News Agency. Tensions between Pyongyang and Seoul over the fate of the joint industrial zone in the North Korean city have been simmering since the north's announcement in March 2008 that it was expelling several South Korean government workers stationed at the facility. Since that time, there have been periodic disruptions of transportation across the border, unilateral revisions of operating regulations by Pyongyang, and threats to close the complex if South Korean firms do not pay more.

The north's actions are about more than money, however.

The Kaesong industrial zone was a centerpiece of inter-Korean economic cooperation. It began operation in 2004 as a result of the 2000 inter-Korean summit. While the project remains far short of some of the estimates of economic activity, it currently hosts some 100 South Korean companies that employ 39,000 North Korean workers in labor-intensive light industry. South Korean companies pay workers' salaries directly to the North Korean government, with total wages remitted to Pyongyang in 2008 amounting to $26.8 million, up from $13.8 million a year earlier, according to statistics from South Korea's Unification Ministry. The average salary in the zone is between $70 and $80 a month, about half of what South Korean companies pay for similar labor in China.

North Korea's demands for re-negotiated contracts have been seen as a desperate attempt to increase the flow of hard currency to the isolated regime. But for Pyongyang, Kaesong is much more a political issue than an economic one. Salary remittances amount to less than one percent of North Korean gross domestic product, and although the cash is certainly useful, North Korea has not adjusted its activities to rely on the payments. China remains North Korea's most significant economic partner. While Pyongyang ran a $1.28 billion trade deficit with China in 2008 (a sixfold increase from the $210 million deficit in 2004), China continues to underwrite part of the North's economy over concerns that a destabilized North Korea is a much bigger problem than the financial cost of sustaining its neighbor.

North Korea views the economic zone — and the concessions it made like opening the border to rail and road traffic — as political gestures, signs of fraternal cooperation between the Koreas. Under the last two South Korean governments, maintaining smooth relations with North Korea was a key policy, something the current Lee Myung Bak government has reassessed. Seoul had viewed economic and infrastructure development in North Korea as critical components of reducing tensions on the Korean Peninsula and preparing North Korea for eventual reunification. Politically in the south, however, the apparently pro-North Korean policies of the previous governments were seen by the then-opposition as excessive, and as damaging to the critical relation with the United States. The Lee government came to power intending to take a stronger stance toward North Korea. Pyongyang has replied by pulling the rug out from under the various cooperative inter-Korean projects.

With the threats regarding Kaesong, North Korea has already kept Seoul from making a final decision on joining the U.S. Proliferation Security Initiative (PSI) — which is largely directed against North Korea — despite pledges by the South Korean government to join if North Korea launched another missile (which the north did in April). Should Kaesong shut down, North Korea would lose $26 million a year as it reseals its border and rethinks one of its development models (this one based on enclosed foreign-invested economic zones to bring in currency without political or social influence).

For the south, the closure of Kaesong would result in an estimated $1 billion loss to the government and businesses, according to the Forum for Inter-Korea Relations, a nongovernmental organization lobbying for labor rights in the economic zone and direct payments to North Korean workers rather than to the North Korean government. But it would also remove one of the only remaining channels for inter-Korean communication, leaving the south with little additional leverage or venues for shaping North Korean behavior. This is something Seoul is concerned about, as it has worked for years to be able to have a clear say at the table in any international discussions on the future of the Korean Peninsula.

Both sides stand to lose if the zone is closed. Pyongyang is betting that the south is more interested in maintaining operations than walking away, and will accede to at least some of the north's economic and political demands. But even if the south does not cooperate, North Korea's leaders have begun a period of re-consolidation as Kim Jong Il balances the various personalities and power centers in the country in preparation for his successor. If the transition period between Kim Il Sung's death in 1994 and Kim Jong Il's final assumption of power three years later is any indication, the north becomes much more insular during periods of political balancing.

The North Korean Nuclear Test and Geopolitical Reality
May 26, 2009

North Korea tested a nuclear device for the second time in two and a half years May 25. Although North Korea's nuclear weapons program continues to be a work in progress, the event is inherently significant. North Korea has carried out the only two nuclear detonations the world has seen in the 21st century. The most recent detonations prior to those were the spate of tests by India and Pakistan in 1998.

Details continue to emerge through analysis of seismographic and other data, and speculation about the precise nature of the atomic device that Pyongyang may now possess carries on, making this a good moment to examine the underlying reality of nuclear weapons. Examining their history, and the lessons that can be drawn from that history, will help us understand what it will really mean if North Korea does indeed join the nuclear club.

Nuclear Weapons in the 20th Century

Even before an atomic bomb was first detonated on July 16, 1945, the scientists and engineers of the Manhattan Project and the U.S. military struggled with the implications of the science they pursued. Ultimately they were driven by a profound sense of urgency to complete the program in time to affect the outcome of the war, meaning that understanding the implications of the atomic bomb was largely a luxury that would have to wait. Even after World War II, the frantic pace of the Cold War kept pushing weapons development forward at a break-neck pace. This meant that in their early days, atomic weapons were probably more advanced than the understanding of their moral and practical utility.

But the promise of nuclear weapons was immense. If appropriate delivery systems could be designed and built, and armed with more powerful nuclear warheads, a nation could continually threaten another country's very means of existence: its people, industry, military installations and governmental institutions. Battlefield or tactical nuclear weapons would make the massing of military formations suicidal — or so military planners once thought. What seemed clear early on was that nuclear weapons had fundamentally changed everything. War was thought to have been made obsolete, simply too dangerous and too destructive to contemplate. Some of the most brilliant minds of the Manhattan Project talked of how atomic weapons made world government necessary.

But perhaps the most surprising aspect of the advent of the nuclear age is how little actually changed. Great power competition continued apace (despite a new, bilateral dynamic). The Soviets blockaded Berlin for nearly a year starting in 1948, in defiance of what was then the world's sole nuclear power: the United States. Likewise, the United States refused to use nuclear weapons in the Korean War (despite the pleas of Gen. Douglas MacArthur) even as Chinese divisions surged across the Yalu River, overwhelming U.S., South Korean and allied forces and driving them back south, reversing the rapid gains of late 1950.

Again and again, the situations nuclear weapons were supposed to deter occurred. The military realities they would supposedly shift simply persisted. Thus, the United States lost in Vietnam. The Syrians and the Egyptians invaded Israel in 1973 (despite knowing that the Israelis had acquired nuclear weapons by that point). The Soviet Union lost in Afghanistan. India and Pakistan went to war in 1999 — and nearly went to war twice after that. In none of these cases was it judged appropriate to risk employing nuclear weapons — nor was it clear what utility they might have.

Enduring Geopolitical Stability

Wars of immense risk are born of desperation. In World War II, both Nazi Germany and Imperial Japan took immense geostrategic gambles — and lost — but knowingly took the risk because of untenable geopolitical circumstances. By comparison, the postwar United States and Soviet Union were geopolitically secure. Washington had come into its own as a global power secured by the buffer of two oceans, while Moscow enjoyed the greatest strategic depth it had ever known.

The U.S.-Soviet competition was, of course, intense, from the nuclear arms race to the space race to countless proxy wars. Yet underlying it was a fear that the other side would engage in a war that was on its face irrational. Western Europe promised the Soviet Union immense material wealth but would likely have been impossible to subdue. (Why should a Soviet leader expect to succeed where Napoleon and Hitler had failed?) Even without nuclear weapons in the calculus, the cost to the Soviets was too great, and fears of the Soviet invasion of Europe along the North European Plain were overblown. The desperation that caused Germany to seek control over Europe twice in the first half of the 20th century simply did not characterize either the Soviet or U.S. geopolitical position even without nuclear weapons in play. It was within this context that the concept of mutually assured destruction emerged — the idea that each side would possess sufficient retaliatory capability to inflict a devastating "second strike" in the event of even a surprise nuclear attack.

Through it all, the metrics of nuclear warfare became more intricate. Throw weights and penetration rates were calculated and recalculated. Targets were assigned and reassigned. A single city would begin to have multiple target points, each with multiple strategic warheads allocated to its destruction. Theorists and strategists would talk of successful scenarios for first strikes. But only in the Cuban Missile Crisis did the two sides really threaten one another's fundamental national interests. There were certainly other moments when the world inched toward the nuclear brink. But each time, the global system found its balance, and there was little cause or incentive for political leaders on either side of the Iron Curtain to so fundamentally alter the status quo as to risk direct military confrontation — much less nuclear war.

So through it all, the world carried on, its fundamental dynamics unchanged by the ever-present threat of nuclear war. Indeed, history has shown that once a country has acquired nuclear weapons, the weapons fail to have any real impact on the country's regional standing or pursuit of power in the international system.

Thus, not only were nuclear weapons never used in even desperate combat situations, their acquisition failed to entail any meaningful shift in geopolitical position. Even as the United Kingdom acquired nuclear weapons in the 1950s, its colonial empire crumbled. The Soviet Union was behaving aggressively all along its periphery before it acquired nuclear weapons. And the Soviet Union had the largest nuclear arsenal in the world when it collapsed — not only despite its arsenal, but in part because the economic burden of creating and maintaining it was unsustainable. Today, nuclear-armed France and non-nuclear armed Germany vie for dominance on the Continent with no regard for France's small nuclear arsenal.

The Intersection of Weapons, Strategy and Politics

This August will mark 64 years since any nation used a nuclear weapon in combat. What was supposed to be the ultimate weapon has proved too risky and too inappropriate as a weapon ever to see the light of day again. Though nuclear weapons certainly played a role in the strategic calculus of the Cold War, they had no relation to a military strategy that anyone could seriously contemplate. Militaries, of course, had war plans and scenarios and target sets. But outside this world of role-play Armageddon, neither side was about to precipitate a global nuclear war.

Clausewitz long ago detailed the inescapable connection between national political objectives and military force and strategy. Under this thinking, if nuclear weapons had no relation to practical military strategy, then they were necessarily disconnected (at least in the Clausewitzian sense) from — and could not be integrated with — national and political objectives in a coherent fashion. True to the theory, despite ebbs and flows in the nuclear arms race, for 64 years, no one has found a good reason to detonate a nuclear bomb.

By this line of reasoning, STRATFOR is not suggesting that complete nuclear disarmament — or "getting to zero" — is either possible or likely. The nuclear genie can never be put back in the bottle. The idea that the world could ever remain nuclear-free is untenable. The potential for clandestine and crash nuclear programs will remain a reality of the international system, and the world's nuclear powers are unlikely ever to trust the rest of the system enough to completely surrender their own strategic deterrents.

Legacy, Peer and Bargaining Programs

The countries in the world today with nuclear weapons programs can be divided into three main categories.

- Legacy Programs: This category comprises countries like the United Kingdom and France that maintain small arsenals even after the end of the threat they acquired them for; in this case, to stave off a Soviet invasion of Western Europe. In the last few years, both London and Paris have decided to sustain their small arsenals in some form for the foreseeable future. This category is also important for highlighting the unlikelihood that a country will surrender its weapons after it has acquired them (the only exceptions being South Africa and several Soviet Republics that repatriated their weapons back to Russia after the Soviet collapse).

- Peer Programs: The original peer program belonged to the Soviet Union, which aggressively and ruthlessly pursued a nuclear weapons capacity following the bombing of Hiroshima and Nagasaki in 1945 because its peer competitor, the United States, had them. The Pakistani and Indian nuclear programs also can be understood as peer programs.

- Bargaining Programs: These programs are about the threat of developing nuclear weapons, a strategy that involves quite a bit of tightrope walking to make the threat of acquiring nuclear weapons appear real and credible while at the same time not making it appear so urgent as to require military intervention. Pyongyang pioneered this strategy, and has wielded it deftly over the years. As North Korea continues to progress with its efforts, however, it will shift from a bargaining chip to an actual program — one it will be unlikely to surrender once it acquires weapons. Iran also falls into this category, though it could also progress to a more substantial program if it gets far enough along. Though parts of its program are indeed clandestine, other parts are actually highly publicized and celebrated as milestones, both to continue to highlight progress internationally and for purposes of domestic consumption. Indeed, manipulating the international community with a nuclear weapon — or even a civilian nuclear program — has proved to be a rare instance of the utility of nuclear weapons beyond simple deterrence.

The Challenges of a Nuclear Weapons Program

Pursuing a nuclear weapons program is not without its risks. Another important distinction is that between a crude nuclear device and an actual weapon. The former requires only that a country demonstrate the capability to initiate an uncontrolled nuclear chain reaction, creating a rather large hole in the ground. That device may be crude, fragile or otherwise temperamental. But this does not automatically imply the capability to mount a rugged and reliable nuclear warhead on a delivery vehicle and send it flying to the other side of the earth. In other words, it does not immediately translate into a meaningful deterrent.

For that, a ruggedized, reliable nuclear weapon must be mated with some manner of reliable delivery vehicle to have real military meaning. After World War II, the B-29's limited range and the few nuclear weapons the United States had on hand meant that its vaunted nuclear arsenal was, at first, extremely difficult to bring to bear against the Soviet heartland. The United States would spend untold resources to overcome this obstacle in the decade that followed.

The modern nuclear weapon is a product not only of physics but also of decades of design work and full-scale nuclear testing. It combines expertise not just in nuclear physics but also in materials science, rocketry, missile guidance and the like. A nuclear device does not come easy. A nuclear weapon is one of the most advanced syntheses of complex technologies ever achieved by man.

Many dangers exist for an aspiring nuclear power. Many of the facilities associated with a clandestine nuclear weapons program are large, fixed and complex. They are vulnerable to airstrikes — as Syria found in 2007. (And though history shows that nuclear weapons are unlikely to be employed, it is still in the interests of other powers to deny that capability to a potential adversary.)

The history of proliferation shows that few countries actually ever decide to pursue nuclear weapons. Obtaining them requires immense investment (the more clandestine the attempt the more costly the program becomes) and the ability to focus and coordinate a major national undertaking over time. It is not something a leader like Venezuela's Hugo Chavez could decide to pursue on a whim. A national government must have cohesion over the long span of time necessary to go from the foundations of a weapons program to a meaningful deterrent capability.

The Exceptions

In addition to this sustained commitment must be the willingness to be suspected by the international community and endure pariah status and isolation — in and of themselves significant risks for even moderately integrated economies. One must also have reasonable means of deterring a pre-emptive strike by a competing power. A Venezuelan weapons program is therefore unlikely because the United States would act decisively the moment one was discovered, and there is little Venezuela could do to deter such action.

North Korea, on the other hand, has held downtown Seoul (just across the demilitarized zone) at risk for generations with one of the highest concentrations of deployed artillery, artillery rockets and short-range ballistic missiles on the planet. From the outside, Pyongyang is perceived as unpredictable enough that any potential pre-emptive strike on its nuclear facilities is too risky not because of some newfound nuclear capability but because of Pyongyang's capability to turn the South Korean capital city into a proverbial "sea of fire" via conventional means. A nuclear North Korea, the world has now seen, is not sufficient alone to risk renewed war on the Korean Peninsula.

Iran is similarly defended. It can threaten to close the Strait of Hormuz, to launch a barrage of medium-range ballistic missiles at Israel, and to use its proxies in Lebanon and elsewhere to respond with a new campaign of artillery rocket fire, guerrilla warfare and terrorism. But the biggest deterrent to a strike on Iran is Tehran's ability to seriously interfere in ongoing U.S. efforts in Iraq and Afghanistan — efforts already tenuous enough without direct Iranian opposition.

In other words, some other deterrent (be it conventional or unconventional) against attack is a prerequisite for a nuclear program, since powerful potential adversaries can otherwise move to halt such efforts. North Korea and Iran have such deterrents. Most other countries widely considered major proliferation dangers — Iraq before 2003, Syria or Venezuela, for example — do not. And that fundamental deterrent remains in place after the country acquires nuclear weapons.

In short, no one was going to invade North Korea — or even launch limited military strikes against it — before its first nuclear test in 2006. And no one will do so now, nor will anyone do so after its next test. So North Korea — with or without nuclear weapons — remains secure from invasion. With or without nuclear weapons, North Korea remains a pariah state, isolated from the international community. And with or without them, the world will go on.

The Global Nuclear Dynamic

Despite how frantic the pace of nuclear proliferation may seem at the moment, the true pace of the global nuclear dynamic is slowing dramatically. With the Comprehensive Test Ban Treaty effectively in place (though it has not been ratified), the pace of nuclear weapons development has already slowed and stabilized. The world's current nuclear powers rely to some degree on the generation of weapons that were validated and certified before testing was banned. They are currently working toward weapons and force structures that will provide them with a stable, sustainable deterrent for the foreseeable future rooted largely in this pre-existing weapons architecture.

New additions to the nuclear club are always cause for concern. But though North Korea's nuclear program continues apace, it hardly threatens to shift underlying geopolitical realities. It may encourage the United States to retain a slightly larger arsenal to reassure Japan and South Korea about the credibility of its nuclear umbrella. It also could encourage Tokyo and Seoul to pursue their own weapons. But none of these shifts, though significant, is likely to alter the defining military, economic and political dynamics of the region in any fundamental way.

Nuclear arms are better understood as an insurance policy, one that no potential aggressor has any intention of steering afoul of. Without practical military or political use, they remain held in reserve — where, in all likelihood, they will remain for the foreseeable future.

Breaking With the Armistice Agreement
May 27, 2009

The North Korean military mission to Panmunjom (which serves as the North Korean liaison for issues dealing with the 1953 Armistice Agreement) declared May 27 that North Korea was no longer bound by the agreement that ended the Korean War. The north claimed that South Korea and the United States had violated the agreement through the U.S.-led Proliferation Security Initiative (PSI), which in part focuses on stopping North Korean vessels involved in the transfer of nuclear or missile technology to other states. South Korea committed its full participation in the PSI following North Korea's May 25 nuclear test.

The North Korean military's announcement, later reiterated by the Committee for the Peaceful Reunification of the Fatherland — which coordinates inter-Korean relations — was coupled with threats that North Korea's military could no longer guarantee the safety of U.S. or South Korean ships or aircraft along the west coast of North Korea. This is an area near the disputed Northern Limit Line, the western maritime extension of the DMZ that divides the two Koreas. The area, a prime crab-fishing ground, saw deadly clashes between North and South Korean naval vessels in 1999 and 2002 (though in 2005 Pyongyang and Seoul signed a new maritime agreement that allows commercial vessels from each country to traverse each other's waters in certain areas).

Pyongyang's latest steps to escalate tensions around the Korean Peninsula serve a dual purpose: one internal, the other external.

Domestically, Pyongyang has been quick to announce and hold rallies around its recent attempted satellite launch and its nuclear test. In part, this show of strength is intended to belie any rumors or information that has trickled into the north related to Kim Jong Il's stroke last year to show that Kim remains firmly in control and unafraid of any foreign interference. The rising military and technological displays are also related to Kim's reshuffling of the north's top leadership, concentrating power further in an expanded National Defense Commission (NDC) as a collective core of future leadership. This group, then, can serve to balance various interest groups in North Korea. It can also provide guidance and support for Kim's successor. It is rumored that Kim may even hand over power to one of his sons — likely the youngest one Kim Jong Un — in 2012, remaining behind the scenes as an elder statesman and relying in part on the NDC to backstop the fledgling leader until he is more capable.

As part of the ramp-up to 2012 (the 100th anniversary of Kim Il Sung's birth), North Korea launched a 150-day economic campaign, running from May 10 to Oct. 10, to rally the nation behind a construction and production boom. Like prior campaigns, this one serves both as an attempt to leap forward in industrial development and as a nationalist rallying point. The nuclear test, coming in the early days of the campaign, serves as a symbol of North Korean strength. It also serves as a reminder of the embattled nature of the regime, as Pyongyang would tell it, to reinforce the need to focus on local capabilities rather than to rely on foreign assistance.

But there is also an external focus to the actions. The announcement of a withdrawal from the 1953 Armistice Agreement in the short term may be intended to apply further pressure on South Korea, but in the longer term it is directed at the United States. When North Korea concludes its current 150-day drive (during which it will likely carry out another long-range missile test and possibly another nuclear test), Pyongyang will once again make itself available for negotiations with the United States. This time, North Korea is looking to shift the topic of talks away from denuclearization and toward the status of relations with the United States.

The Armistice Agreement was technically only a cease-fire, not a peace accord, and South Korea is not even a signatory to the deal, choosing at the time not to accept a divided Korea by signing. By claiming the Armistice Agreement is now null and void, Pyongyang first and foremost brings the question of war or peace to the negotiating table with Washington. North Korea does not want to talk nuclear disarmament. Instead, it wants to talk normalization of relations. The nuclear program, while serving as a useful tool for encouraging negotiations, has thus distracted from Pyongyang's main intent.

When Kim Jong Il is more confident of his re-arrangements of the elite in Pyongyang, and when the current 150-day drive is complete, North Korea will again open channels for dialogue. It will focus primarily on bilateral talks with the United States, not the multilateral six-party format. Pyongyang had tried to time its 2003 nuclear crisis to force a replacement of the Armistice Agreement around the 50th anniversary of the end of the Korean War. But it failed for multiple reasons, not least of which was the misreading of U.S. security views following the 9/11 attacks. Pyongyang is now looking at a new symbolic date, the 60th anniversary of the start of the Korean War next June. And this time, North Korea intends to make sure the stakes are higher and the focus is centered on the status of the peace accord.

Crises as Political Ploys
Sept. 4, 2009

In a Sept. 3 letter to the U.N. Security Council, North Korea announced it has almost completed experimental uranium extraction and continues to weaponize plutonium from its Yongbyon nuclear reactor. In the same message, Pyongyang said it was prepared for sanctions or dialogue. The message was timed to match U.S. nuclear envoy Stephen Bosworth's visit to Asia, and follows North Korea's pattern to create crises in order to pave the way for dialogue.

Pyongyang's letter to the United Nations balanced threatening rhetoric about new nuclear weapons development with a call for the resumption of dialogue. Since the early 1990s, when the Cold War system collapsed and Pyongyang found itself standing alone against the United States, Pyongyang has employed a dual-track policy of creating crises with the intent to negotiate back down to the status quo, and gain concessions along the way. For North Korea, the concessions are not as important as the broader goal — maintaining the regime. And this Pyongyang has done remarkably well, despite deep-seated economic problems, international condemnation and pressure and a charter position on the U.S. Axis of Evil list.

North Korea has steadily escalated the sense of crisis this year, detaining two U.S. journalists in March, carrying out a second nuclear test May 25 — and two days later declaring itself no longer bound by the Armistice Agreement — and carrying out a series of missile tests between July 2 and July 4. But in recent weeks, Pyongyang appeared to step back from confrontation, hosting former U.S. President Bill Clinton in early August and releasing the U.S. journalists, hosting South Korean representatives of Hyundai, re-opening the border crossing to the Kaesong joint economic zone and sending representatives to Seoul for the funeral of former South Korean President Kim Dae Jung.

The latest letter once again raises tensions, with Pyongyang claiming not only to be preparing additional nuclear weapons but also to be pursuing uranium enrichment (an accusation that in 2002 triggered a several-year nuclear crisis). Pyongyang's Yongbyon reactor — which the country shut down as part of its negotiations with the United States and others — is a plutonium reactor, and purifying weapons-grade plutonium is somewhat simpler than purifying uranium, as it uses a simpler chemical process rather than a four-stage process that includes complex cascades of centrifuges .

However, creating a plutonium-based nuclear weapon is more complex, requiring a perfectly timed and perfectly placed set of explosive charges around a sphere of plutonium that detonate at the exact moment with the exact force, triggering fission. This implosion device requires much finer skill and quality control than the simpler uranium-based gun-type device that essentially fires one piece of uranium into another, the force of the collision triggering the reaction.

If North Korea is experimenting with uranium enrichment, it is probably not with the use of centrifuges but in laboratory tests with laser isotope separation. Thus, at this stage, it is highly unlikely that Pyongyang has enough weaponized uranium to create even a single nuclear device. Rather, it is simply sending a message that there is more to deal with in resolving the North Korean situation. It is very common for Pyongyang to add one or two additional elements into the mix shortly before restarting dialogue, making the new items the top priority for resolution. When it works, Pyongyang gives up something it does not even really have (or at least not functionally), and in return receives money, fuel, food and time.

Pyongyang has a history of arranging crises and launching both the stressors and talks at times of its own choosing. North Korea has set the resumption of dialogue for around October, after the country completes a 150-day mass economic campaign. Starting the new crisis now puts them on track.

By announcing the uranium enrichment now, as Bosworth travels to Asia to meet with his partners in dealing with the North Korean nuclear crisis, Pyongyang can stir confusion and disagreement among the partners and later exploit these differences. In addition, by raising the stakes right after making more friendly gestures, North Korea leaves many arguing that the regime is desperate for dialogue and whether dialogue, sanctions or more concrete action are necessary.

This places Washington in a no-win situation. If it tries to simply ignore North Korea, Pyongyang can exploit the concerns of its neighbors and the international media to pressure U.S. action. Washington is unlikely to try a more permanent solution via military means, leaving a continuation of the U.S. program to target sanctions and dialogue. This also creates political problems, not only in the potential example it sets for U.S. nuclear policy toward Iran (and Washington has tried to distinguish between the two as separate cases), but also in perpetuating the seemingly never-ending cycle of North Korean provocation and appeasement.

Pyongyang's Continued Push for Peace with Washington
Feb. 16, 2010

North Korea marked 68-year-old leader Kim Jong Il's Feb. 16 birthday with several days of celebrations, rallies, flower shows and speeches. In one speech, Kim Yong Nam — president of the Presidium of the Supreme People's Assembly, North Korea's second-in-command and nominal head of government — re-emphasized

Pyongyang's desire for an end to the "hostile relations" between North Korea and the United States, calling for dialogue and negotiations with Washington. The comments are part of a coordinated government campaign to reshape the focus of U.S.-North Korean relations, focusing on what Pyongyang has identified as an even more fundamental issue than the status of North Korea's nuclear program: the replacement of the 1953 Armistice Agreement with a formal peace accord. Only then, according to North Korea, can denuclearization talks achieve success.

North Korea has long urged the replacement of the Armistice Agreement with a formal peace treaty. In some ways, this has been an underlying element of the nuclear talks all along. From the most basic of North Korean perspectives, the nuclear issue has been one of ensuring regime survival, and the main threat seen to that survival has been the United States, particularly since the end of the Cold War system of international relations. While Washington perceives North Korea as an unreliable negotiator, constantly going back on agreed-upon deals, Pyongyang views the United States in the same light, and changes in U.S. presidential administrations seem to return any prior negotiations to their starting point. For North Korea, one key way to stabilize the issue is through a formal peace accord.

With much of the ambiguity and uncertainty of policies on both sides tempered, so the theory goes, Pyongyang can then move forward with some of its economic experiments without the constant fear of the United States waiting to pounce on any perceived weakness or crack in North Korea. But perhaps even more pressing this time around for North Korea is the preparation for a domestic leadership transition — most likely between Kim Jong Il and his youngest son, Kim Jong Un. This is tentatively set to take place around 2012 and, to ensure greater stability, will be a live transfer of power, with Kim Jong Il stepping down but maintaining control from behind the scenes. This is to avoid the uncertainties and internal struggles triggered by the 1994 death of Kim Il Sung, with Kim Jong Il — despite being the long-appointed successor — taking more than three years to finally solidify his rule.

In 1994, Kim Il Sung was using the nuclear crisis to force the United States into negotiations and ultimately a normalization of relations, breaking Pyongyang out of the constraints left over from the end of the Cold War. Kim Jong Il was unable to capitalize on the groundwork, however, as he did not have his father's heft of authority in changing North Korea's political rhetoric and actions. And although the Agreed Framework was signed in 1994, a planned inter-Korean summit did not take place until 2000, and the replacement of the Armistice Agreement with the United States remained unfulfilled. Kim Jong Il is now working to bring about the peace accord before his transfer of power, and his illness has only emphasized the need to take action sooner rather than later.

In May 2009, North Korea's military mission to the United Nations declared it was no longer bound by the Armistice Agreement. In October 2009, as North Korea was completing a 150-day economic campaign, it began telegraphing the necessity of replacing the Armistice Agreement as a prerequisite to resuming the long-stalled nuclear talks. This was reinforced later in the month when Ri Gun, one of Pyongyang's chief nuclear negotiators, visited New York and California. The issue was repeated throughout November 2009 in North Korean media (even amid a brief naval clash between North and South Korea). In December 2009, North Korea made it clear during U.S. Special Envoy for North Korea Stephen Bosworth's visit to Pyongyang that the resumption of six-party nuclear talks, or any chance for North Korean denuclearization, would first require movement toward a peace accord. This was in line with the Sept. 19 Agreement, reached in 2005, that included the replacement of the Armistice Agreement as a major element of the overall negotiation process.

In its Jan. 1 New Year joint editorial, North Korea made the establishment of a "lasting peace system" on the Korean Peninsula one of its stated priorities. This was expanded and made official on Jan. 11, when the Foreign Ministry issued a statement saying it was "essential to conclude a peace treaty for terminating the state of war, a root cause of hostile relations." Pyongyang blamed the cyclical nature of the years-long nuclear talks to the lack of trust between the two main players and said progress could only be made through building confidence, and confidence could only come through the establishment of a peace accord. Within days, the North Korean embassies in China and Russia held press conferences on the initiative, urging backing from those countries.

On Jan. 21, North Korea upped the ante, warning that the lack of a peace accord meant that the situation on the Korean Peninsula could erupt into war at any moment, triggered by the slightest provocation or misunderstanding. Perhaps to drive home the point, North Korean shore batteries carried out a series of artillery exercises near the North Limit Line from Jan. 26 to Jan. 29, the first salvo triggering a live-fire response from South Korea. At the conclusion of the exercises, North Korean official media again urged the United States to swiftly enter into negotiations to replace the Armistice Agreement, adding the incentive that the conclusion of the peace accord would pave the way for the swift resolution of the nuclear issue.

What is interesting about the North Korean statements on the peace accord this year is that the tone lacks some of the excessive rhetoric and exaggerated bellicosity of past years. This shift in tone appears to convey a seriousness on Pyongyang's part, an urgency and insistence to deal with this issue first — and to emphasize that this is the real core issue for North Korea. A nuclear deterrent is there to ensure North Korea is not vulnerable to U.S. hostility, but if Washington makes a concrete move to end hostility, Pyongyang will see less of a need to maintain its nuclear deterrent. And the request for a peace accord is also more realistic than previous calls for the United States to withdraw its troops from South Korea as a symbolic gesture of nonaggression.

With the 2012 deadline approaching, Pyongyang is looking to resolve a major foreign relations issue before dealing with the potential uncertainties of a leadership transition. Since his illness, Kim Jong Il has reasserted his authority at home and shifted around the military and political leadership, and now he is looking to fulfill a major North Korean imperative: securing the nation from an ever-present external threat. While the nuclear program offers a temporary solution, Pyongyang is seeking something more lasting, something that will not shift with each political transition in Washington and will also serve to reduce North Korea's strong dependence on, and thus vulnerability to, neighboring China.

Pyongyang has opened a window of opportunity for resolution, but the issue of trust goes both ways, and Washington has seen little indication of North Korea's reliability. But there is a clear shift in North Korean rhetoric and a flurry of behind-the-scenes discussions taking place among North Korea, the United States, South Korea, Japan, China and Russia, and the situation bears close attention.

South Korean Warship Sunk in the Yellow Sea
March 26, 2010

The South Korean government has convened an emergency Cabinet meeting in the wake of what may have been a hostile sinking of a South Korean warship in the Yellow Sea on March 26.

Though details are still unconfirmed, it appears that the 1,200-ton corvette ChonAn (772) suffered a catastrophic explosion in its stern and sunk rapidly at 9:45 p.m. local time. Reports suggest that many of the 104 sailors aboard the ship, which was patrolling in waters southwest of Baengnyeong Island at the time of the explosion, are feared dead.

Though there is no shortage of causes for explosions on a modern warship (the ChonAn has a 76mm naval gun at her stern) and accidents do happen, the South Korean navy is a professional force and the rapidity of the sinking despite a full complement to conduct damage control is certainly striking.

In addition, the ChonAn's sister ship, SukCho (778), reportedly fired on an unidentified vessel leaving the area following the explosion.

THE CHONAN INCIDENT, MARCH 26, 2010

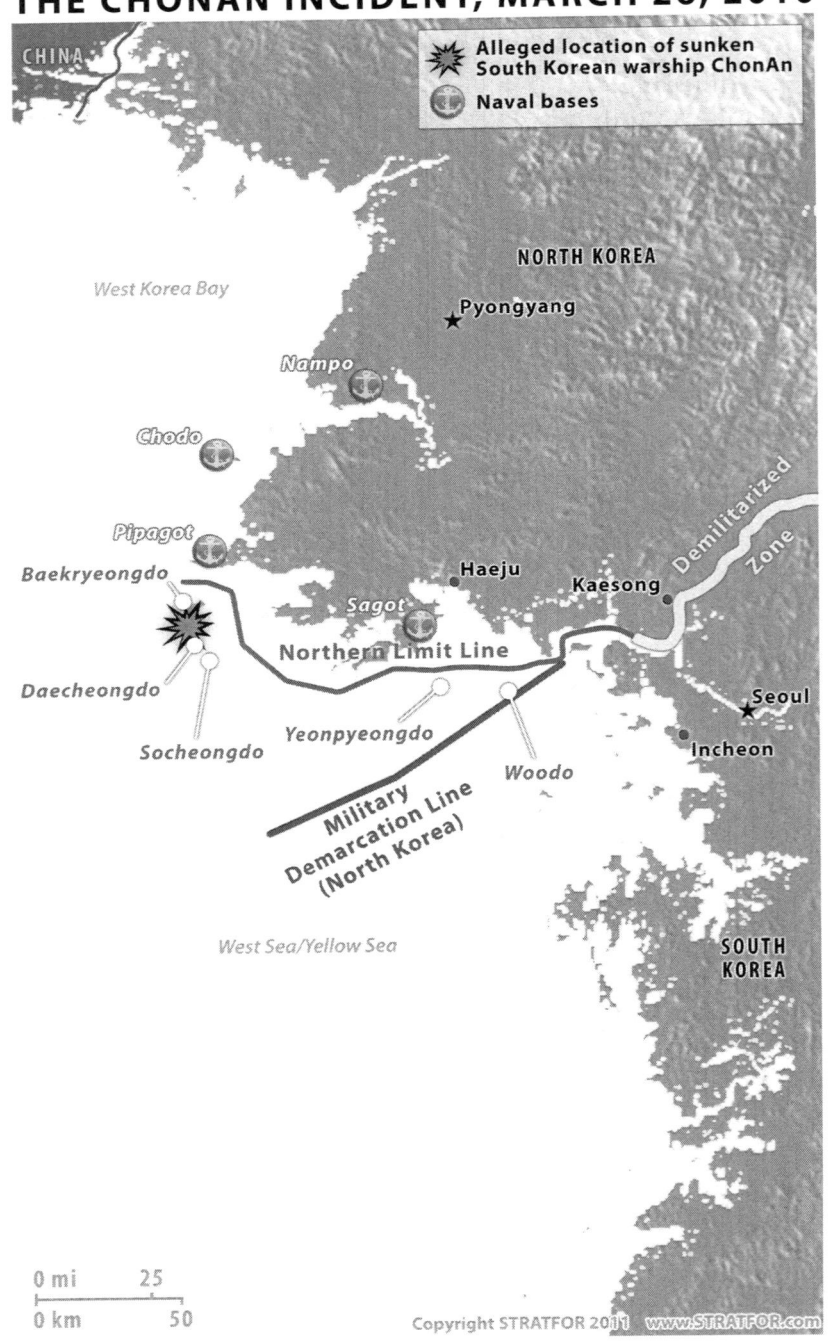

Alleged location of sunken South Korean warship ChonAn

Naval bases

CHINA

West Korea Bay

NORTH KOREA

Pyongyang

Nampo

Chodo

Pipagot

Baekryeongdo

Haeju

Kaesong

Sagot

Demilitarized Zone

Northern Limit Line

Daecheongdo

Socheongdo

Yeonpyeongdo

Woodo

Seoul

Incheon

Military Demarcation Line (North Korea)

West Sea/Yellow Sea

SOUTH KOREA

0 mi   25

0 km   50

Copyright STRATFOR 2011   www.STRATFOR.com

The combination of these details — though unconfirmed at this time — certainly raise the possibility that hostile action by North Korea could have been involved.

Furthermore, the location of the attack, in hotly contested waters off the Korean Peninsula, raises the likelihood that the event is related to tensions between South and North Korea. While naval clashes are not entirely uncommon in this area, the deliberate sinking of a surface combatant of this magnitude would be extremely significant.

North Korea: Managing the Aftermath of the ChonAn Incident
May 24, 2010

North Korean Minister of the People's Armed Forces, Vice Marshal Kim Yong Chun, issued a statement May 22 via official media condemning South Korea's refusal to allow a team of North Korean inspectors to visit South Korea to assess the evidence Seoul prepared during the investigation of the March 26 sinking of the navy corvette ChonAn. Kim, also a vice chairman of the National Defense Commission (NDC), the center of political power in North Korea, demanded Seoul allow the NDC team to visit. He cited Chapter 2, Article 10 of the 1992 Basic Agreement between Seoul and Pyongyang, which states, "South and North Korea shall resolve peacefully, through dialogue and negotiation, any differences of views and disputes arising between them."

North Korea has strongly denied any involvement in the sinking, becoming even more vociferous as the May 20 announcement of the multinational team's investigation neared. During a May 3-7 visit to Beijing by North Korean leader Kim Jong Il, North Korean officials told the Chinese that Pyongyang was not responsible for the incident, though later Chinese reports suggested that Kim Jong Il himself had remained silent on the issue. While it may seem minor, this point

105

allows North Korea some leeway in dealing with the issue and with its ally, China, as whatever path North Korea takes, Kim's silence means that he did not directly lie to the Chinese president.

Ambiguity in the midst of strong denial is an important part of the North Korean strategy. Pyongyang remains capable of pulling out a surprise card at any moment; in 2002, Kim Jong Il surprised visiting Japanese Prime Minister Junichiro Koizumi by admitting that North Korean agents had kidnapped Japanese citizens in the past, and letting some return to Japan — this despite years of vehement denials of such kidnappings. The North may be holding in reserve a similar surprise admission for the South regarding the ChonAn — a card to play if the timing appears right.

After Kim Jong Il's visit to Beijing, two unusual statements emerged from North Korea that have stirred speculation in the South and elsewhere. On May 14, North Korean media announced that NDC member and First Vice Minister of the People's Armed Forces Kim Il Chol was relieved of all his posts a day earlier due to his "advanced age of 80." Four days later, North Korean state media announced that the Supreme People's Assembly (SPA) would hold another session on June 7.

Kim Il Chol's dismissal was particularly odd. North Korea does not have mandatory retirement, and Kim Il Chol is younger than at least two other members of the NDC. A former commanding officer of the Korean People's Navy, Kim Il Chol reportedly helped engineer the 1968 North Korean capture of the USS Pueblo, a ship that still sits in the Taedong River in Pyongyang as a trophy of North Korean victories over the United States. He was one of Kim Jong Il's allies during his rise to power after the 1994 death of North Korean President Kim Il Sung and was promoted to vice marshal in 1997 during a wave of promotions that solidified Kim Jong Il's power.

There were signs of problems with Kim Il Chol in Pyongyang in early 2009, before the ChonAn incident. He was demoted from his position as minister of the People's Armed Forces and given the more ceremonial role of first vice minister. He was also demoted from an NDC vice chairmanship to a councilor. Both moves could havett reflected internal bickering over Kim Jong Il's succession plans. His dismissal now, in the midst of the ChonAn incident, could reflect disagreements within North Korea's elite over the ChonAn incident and the best way to deal with the fallout. It could also indicate that Pyongyang is using Kim Il Chol as a potential scapegoat for the rising tensions with the South. That would fit with the demand South Korean President Lee Myung Bak made in his May 24 address to the nation, in which he called on North Korea to apologize and punish those responsible for the sinking if the North wanted to get inter-Korean relations back on track. Whatever the reason for the dismissal, Kim Il Chol may find himself punished for the ChonAn incident if the North wants to exploit the South Korean opening.

The SPA session is also unusual, as North Korea rarely calls two sessions in the same year, and the last SPA meeting was in April. SPA sessions usually include a focus on major policy initiatives, particularly economic, and often involve announcements of changes in government positions. With additional sanctions coming, and inter-Korean trade and economic cooperation collapsing (aside from the Kaesong project, which itself may be in jeopardy from the North), Pyongyang could be preparing to announce a new economic direction — one that likely will depend even more on Chinese investment and trade.

China has attempted to appear neutral on the ChonAn incident, though in doing so it has by default backed the North Korean position. It may seem unusual that Beijing would back a net drain on its economic resources, rather than support South Korea, which is a major source of investment in China and accounts for nearly 60 times more trade than does North Korea. However, Beijing is not too concerned about South Korea shutting down trade and investment. Although China is the coordinator of the six-party nuclear talks on North Korea, and ostensibly supports inter-Korean cooperation, Beijing is concerned that Korean reunification or a North Korean collapse would undermine Beijing's ability to use North Korea not only as a lever in international and regional relations (as Beijing is the only country with close ties to North Korea that can influence

Pyongyang's behavior), but would also lead to the loss of the strategic buffer North Korea has served as for the past six decades. By sticking close to North Korea in a time of crisis, Beijing can strengthen its hold over North Korea and potentially influence the direction of the leadership succession.

The SPA session is likely to raise new economic policies linked to Chinese initiatives offered during Kim Jong Il's Beijing visit. For Pyongyang, this means more reliance on a single power — something Pyongyang is loath to accept for long, but in the short term would render moot international moves toward more sanctions. Without China's backing, the United Nations can take little substantial action. Pyongyang also hopes that greater access to North Korean resources and industry will persuade Beijing to push for the resumption of international dialogue on North Korea rather than isolation, as Beijing does not want its own industry or financial system caught in sanctions targeting specific North Korean regime elements, as happened in the Banco Delta Asia incident.

For the North, the issue now is one of managing the fallout and positioning for the future. Pyongyang was already reducing its economic interaction with South Korea as it effectively shut down the Mount Kumgang tourism project and threatened the Kaesong joint economic zone. Further sanctions from the South will not necessarily have a major effect, particularly if China can make up the difference. At the same time, with the South threatening to respond to every new North Korean provocation by exercising its "right of self-defense," and the North threatening the same, the United States and other powers are calling for restraint from both sides, meaning that gestures on the part of the North may lead to a resumption of dialogue, rather than complete isolation or military action.

This comes back to the NDC's demand for access to the investigation and evidence. First, by invoking the Basic Agreement, Pyongyang is offering to reshape this as an inter-Korean issue, rather than an international one. Second, the North is showing it wants to continue engaging the South and that there is room for dialogue rather than immediate confrontation. Finally, the North may be looking for a way to use the evidence to shift blame from the regime to a "rogue element" responsible for the sinking, should it eventually be considered expedient to surprise South Korea — perhaps closer to 2012, when the North is expected to formalize its succession plans and, more importantly, when the South will hold both presidential and parliamentary elections that Pyongyang might hope to influence.

North Korea's Unpredictable Behavior
Aug. 27, 2010

North Korean leader Kim Jong Il is in China. Maybe. Neither Pyongyang nor Beijing have admitted as much, though South Korean media, citing government officials, are reporting that Kim's special train passed into China overnight on Wednesday, and that the rarely traveling North Korean leader visited a middle school in Jilin province on Thursday afternoon. South Korean media and analysts speculate Kim will not visit Beijing, though he is likely to meet with Chinese officials.

The timing of Kim's trip is odd for several reasons. First, Kim visited China some three months ago. Such a rapid return visit is far from the norm for the North's Dear Leader. Second, Kim left for China while former U.S. President Jimmy Carter was in Pyongyang on a mission to free a detained U.S. citizen who had crossed illegally into North Korea. It was widely anticipated that Kim and Carter would meet, and there are reports that Carter has decided to extend his visit to the North, perhaps hoping Kim will return before Carter leaves.

Finally, the visit follows a series of unusual events surrounding North Korea, including the mysterious crash of a North Korean fighter jet in northern China, the return to government of former North Korean Premier (and erstwhile economic reformer) Pak Pong Ju, and the upcoming special meeting of the Workers' Party of Korea, where it is expected that Kim will finally announce his youngest son as his heir apparent.

There is much speculation surrounding the purpose of Kim's purported trip: to gain China's support for the North Korean leadership transition (some media suggests Kim's youngest, Kim Jong Un, is along for the ride), to ask China for substantial economic aid needed in part because of recent flooding, to discuss changes in strategy for the six-party nuclear talks, to seek emergency medical care, or to discuss significant upcoming shifts in North Korean economic and foreign policies. It may be any one or a combination of these, but for Kim to make the effort to leave North Korea, particularly at a time when a former head of state of the United States is in Pyongyang, appears highly significant.

Carter's visit to Pyongyang was months in the planning, and it was not a surprise to the North Korean leadership. Kim's travels abroad normally entail weeks if not months of preparation to ensure security along whatever route he takes, and to make sure there are no potential issues that may arise in Pyongyang while Kim is out of the country. Thus, barring some very strange — and highly improbable — lack of communication in North Korea, or some tremendously important and unexpected issue, it would appear Kim either timed his trip out of the country to coincide with Carter's visit, or allowed Carter's visit in spite of Kim's brief absence.

Kim's infrequent trips abroad often relate to major adjustments in North Korean economic and foreign policy, and usually include a final coordination with China or, on occasion, Russia, to ensure support from a friendly sponsor state. There have been signals from Pyongyang — directly and via China and other parties — that North Korea is preparing to return soon to multilateral talks about the North Korean nuclear program, though that shouldn't require Kim to visit China to coordinate efforts. It may be that the North is looking for assurances and cooperation should it change its stance on the sinking of the South Korean navy corvette ChonAn earlier this year. Given China's staunch support of its ally's innocence in the succeeding months, Pyongyang needs to tread carefully so as not to embarrass Beijing.

Whatever the reason, it remains a fact that Jimmy Carter is in Pyongyang, apparently patiently awaiting a meeting with Kim Jong Il, although the latter has stepped out of the country for a bit. In 1994, Carter paid a visit to North Korea, much to then-President Bill Clinton's chagrin at the time, and served as a conduit for North Korean founder and leader Kim Il Sung to defuse a nuclear crisis that nearly triggered U.S. airstrikes on North Korea. The Carter visit also gave Kim Il Sung the opportunity to call for a summit meeting with then-South Korean President Kim Young Sam (a meeting that never took place due to the elder Kim Il Sung's death), and to shape North Korea's image abroad.

While there are no immediate signs that the younger Kim is about to follow in his father's footsteps with elder statesman Carter, even for those familiar with North Korea's often carefully choreographed "unpredictable" behavior, the current situation seems outside North Korea's pattern. Thus, it is notable as much for what we don't know as for what we do.

Is North Korea Moving Another 'Red Line'?
Nov. 23, 2010

North Korea and South Korea exchanged artillery fire near the Northern Limit Line (NLL), their disputed western border in the Yellow Sea/West Sea, on Nov. 23. The incident damaged as many as 100 homes and thus far has killed two South Korean soldiers with several others, including some civilians, wounded. The South Korean government convened an emergency Cabinet meeting soon after the incident and called for the prevention of escalation. It later warned of "stern retaliation" if North Korea launches additional attacks. Pyongyang responded by threatening to launch additional

ARTILLERY EXCHANGES, NOV. 23, 2010

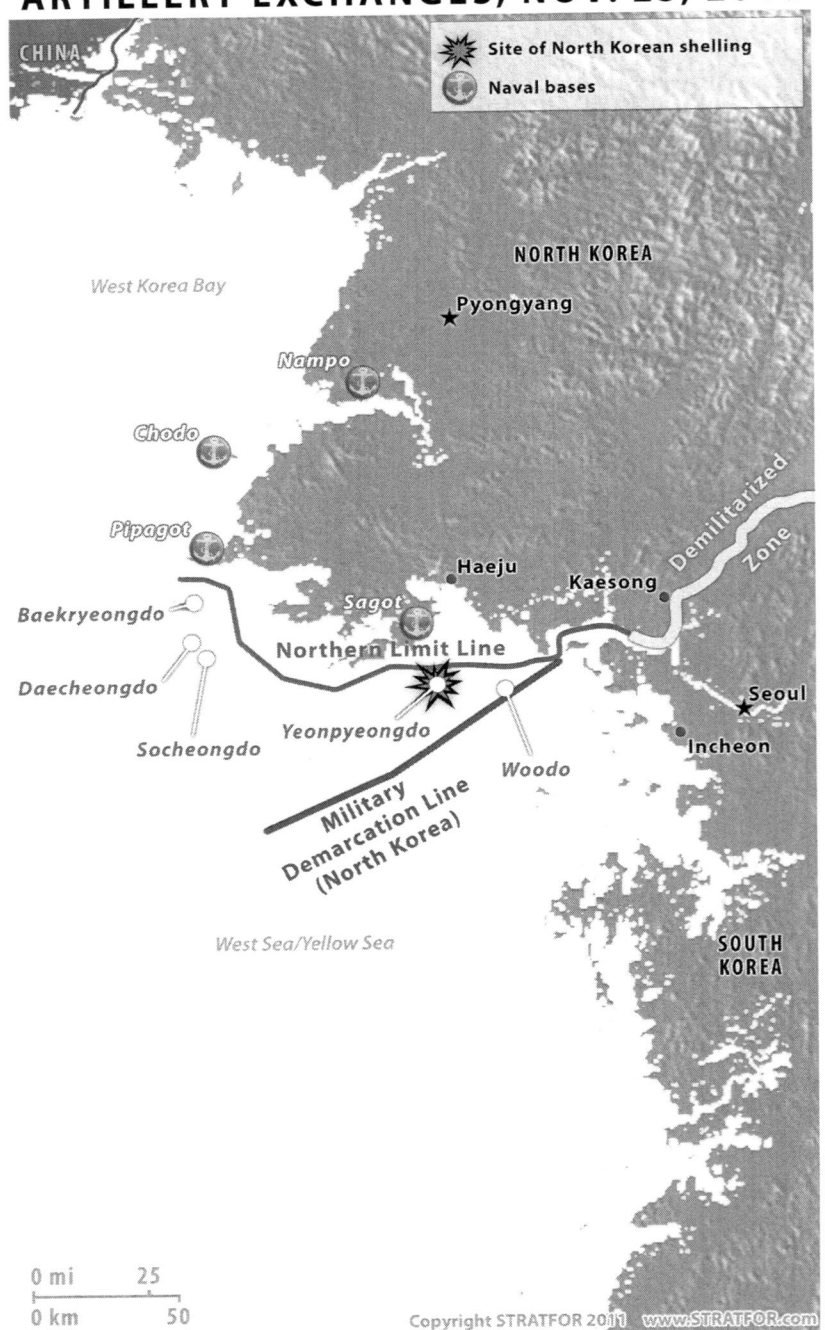

Site of North Korean shelling

Naval bases

CHINA

West Korea Bay

NORTH KOREA

Pyongyang

Nampo

Chodo

Pipagot

Haeju

Kaesong

Demilitarized Zone

Sagot

Baekryeongdo

Northern Limit Line

Daecheongdo

Yeonpyeongdo

Seoul

Socheongdo

Woodo

Incheon

Military Demarcation Line (North Korea)

West Sea/Yellow Sea

SOUTH KOREA

0 mi   25
0 km   50

Copyright STRATFOR 2011   www.STRATFOR.com

strikes, and accused South Korea and the United States of planning to invade North Korea, in reference to the joint Hoguk military exercises currently under way in different locations across South Korea.

The incident is the latest in a series of provocations by Pyongyang near the NLL this year following the sinking of the South Korean warship ChonAn in March. Over the past several years, the NLL has been a major hotspot. While most border incidents have been low-level skirmishes, such as the November 2009 naval episode, a steady escalation of hostilities culminated in the sinking of the ChonAn. The Nov. 23 attack on the South Korean island of Yeonpyeong represents another escalation; similar shellings in the past were for show and often merely involved shooting into the sea, but this attack targeted a military base. It also comes amid an atmosphere of higher tensions surrounding the revelation of active North Korean uranium enrichment facilities, South Korea's disavowal of its Sunshine Policy of warming ties with the North and an ongoing power succession in Pyongyang.

Over the years, North Korea has slowly moved the "red line" regarding its missile program and nuclear development. It was always said that North Korea would never test a nuclear weapon because it would cross a line that the United States had set. Yet North Korea did test a nuclear weapon in October 2006, and then another in May 2009, without facing any dire consequences. This indicates that the red line for the nuclear program either was moved or was rhetorical. The main question after the Nov. 23 attack is whether Pyongyang is attempting to move the red line for conventional attacks. If North Korea is attempting to raise the threshold for a response to such action, it could be playing a very dangerous game.

However, the threat North Korea's nuclear program poses is more theoretical than the threat posed by conventional weapons engagements. Just as it seems that a North Korean nuclear test would not result in military action, the ChonAn sinking and the Nov. 23 attack seem to show that an "unprovoked" North Korean attack also will not lead to military retaliation. If this pattern holds, it means North Korea could decide to move from sea-based to land-based clashes, shell border positions across the Demilitarized Zone or take any number of other actions that are certainly not theoretical.

The questions STRATFOR is focusing on after the Nov. 23 attack are these:

- Is North Korea attempting to test or push back against limits on conventional attacks? If so, are these attacks meant to test South Korea and its allies ahead of an all-out military action, or is the North seeking a political response as it has with its nuclear program? If the former, we must reassess North Korea's behavior and ascertain whether the North Koreans are preparing to take military action against South Korea — perhaps trying to seize one or more of the five South Korean islands along the NLL. If the latter, then at what point will they actually cross a red line that will trigger a response?

- Is South Korea content to constantly redefine "acceptable" North Korean actions? Does South Korea see something in the North that we do not? The South Koreans have good awareness of what is going on in North Korea, and vice versa. The two sides are having a conversation about something and using limited conventional force to get a point across. We should focus on what the underlying issue is.

- What is it that South Korea is afraid of in the North? North Korea gives an American a guided tour of a uranium enrichment facility, then fires across the NLL a couple of days after the news breaks. The South does not respond. It seems that South Korea is afraid of either real power or real weakness in the North, but we do not know which.

7995622R0

Made in the USA
Charleston, SC
28 April 2011